ladies first

WOMEN ATHLETES
WHO MADE A DIFFERENCE

ladies first

WOMEN ATHLETES
WHO MADE A DIFFERENCE

Ken Rappoport

Ω
PEACHTREE
ATLANTA

Ω

Published by
PEACHTREE PUBLISHERS
1700 Chattahoochee Avenue
Atlanta, Georgia 30318-2112

www.peachtree-online.com

First trade paperback edition published in February 2010

Printed in February 2010 in the United States of America by RR Donnelly Book Publishing Services, Bloomsburg, PA

Cover design by Maureen Withee
Book design by Melanie McMahon Ives
Photo research by Ana L. Parker

Photo credits: pp. 3, 8, 13, 23, 27, 35, 39, 59, 65, 71, 78, 81, 86, 91, 95, 101, 106, 111, 115, 121, 124—Associated Press/World Wide Sports; p. 44—Al Brodsky; pp. 49, 55—Shirley Muldowney; pp. 131, 138—Orwell Moore.

10 9 8 7 6 5 4 3 2 (hardcover)
10 9 8 7 6 5 4 3 2 1 (trade paperback)

Library of Congress Cataloging-in-Publication Data

Rappoport, Ken.
  Ladies First : women athletes who made a difference / written by Ken Rappoport.-- 1st ed.
      p. cm.
  Includes bibliographical references.
  ISBN 978-1-56145-338-2 / 1-56145-338-2 (hardcover)
  ISBN 978-1-56145-534-8 / 1-56145-534-2 (trade paperback)
1. Women athletes--Biography--Juvenile literature. 2. Sports for women--History--Juvenile literature. I. Title.

  GV697 .A1R325 2005
  796'.082'0922--dc22   2004026979

For Bernice, my North Star, the light that leads me home

*My thanks to Lisa Banim
for bringing me in to Peachtree Publishers,
to Kathy Landwehr for her warm welcome,
and to Vicky Holifield for her professional and sensitive editing.
And, as always, thanks to my favorite editor at home, Bernice.*

Contents

Introduction 1

1—Gertrude Ederle "Against All Odds" 3
   1920s: Swimming

2—Babe Didrikson Zaharias "The Other Babe" 13
   1930s–50s: Track and Field, Golf

3—Susan Butcher "The Magnificent Musher" 27
   1990s: Dog Sled Racing

4—Julie Krone "The Horse Whisperer" 39
   1990s: Horse Racing

5—Shirley Muldowney "Driving into History" 49
   1970s–80s: Drag Racing

6—Billie Jean King "Serving One Up for Women's Rights" ...59
   1970s: Tennis

7—Wilma Rudolph "The Clarksville Comet" 71
   1950s: Track and Field

8—Joan Benoit Samuelson "Marathon Woman" 81
   1980s: Marathon Running

9—Sonya Henie "The Ice Queen" 91
   1920s–30s: Ice Skating

10—Althea Gibson "The Jackie Robinson of Tennis" 101

    1940s–50s: Tennis

11—Nadia Comaneci "The Perfect Gymnast" 111

    1970s: Gymnastics

12—Manon Rheaume "Manon the Warrior".......................121

    1990s: Hockey

13—All-American Red Heads "A Team of Their Own"......131

    1930s–1980s: Basketball

Conclusion 141

Bibliographical Note..145

About the Author..147

INTRODUCTION

In the 1800s, most sports were off-limits to women. People believed that engaging in strenuous sports was just plain unladylike. In addition, they thought that girls' bodies were much too fragile to withstand the rigors of athletics, and their "nerves" or mental capacities were too weak to handle the pressure of competition. When the first modern Olympic Games were held in 1896, the organizers decided that women should not be allowed to participate.

A great many women did not agree with this attitude. More and more of them had already begun to challenge the traditional roles assigned to females; they had worked to gain voting rights for themselves, and they were entering the work force in growing numbers. The time had come to challenge the traditional roles of women in sports, too.

The turn of the century began a new chapter in women's athletics. In the 1900 Olympic Games in Paris, France, eleven women were allowed to participate in tennis and golf. Charlotte Cooper, a tennis player from England, was the first woman to become an Olympic champion.

Pioneering twentieth-century athletes like Gertrude Ederle, Susan Butcher, and Julie Krone proved that sports was no longer a "man's world." Ederle was the first woman to swim the English Channel, Butcher was among the first of her sex to compete in the Iditarod dog sled race through the Alaskan wilderness, and Krone was one of the first important female jockeys.

This book tells the stories of women who made a lasting impact on sports and society. These First Ladies of Sports all defied the general thinking that women are the "weaker sex." With their amazing achievements, they all forged their special place in history.

And they all shared the same qualities that define any great athlete, male or female: courage, perseverance, and dedication.

1
GERTRUDE EDERLE
Against All Odds

Standing on French soil at Cape Gris-Nez, her heart pounding, Gertrude Ederle surveyed the gray skies and turbulent water. Back in America, a nation waited and wondered. Could she do it?

It was the Roaring Twenties, and a time for great individual expression. Anything went, from flagpole sitters to plucky pilots performing death-defying stunts — and swimmers attempting to cross the English Channel.

But in the 1920s, a female

Ederle at a beach on Long Island, NY, in 1923

swimmer crossing the Channel seemed to be one of the most outrageous stunts of all. Few people believed the "weaker sex" had the strength or stamina to do it.

Only five swimmers had mastered the Channel up to that point—all men. In 1923, Enrique Tiraboschi had set the world record in 16 hours, 33 minutes. Women swimmers had tried the crossing, but they had come up short time and again. In 1925, Ederle had been one of the failures. Now she was about to try it again.

When Ederle prepared to take the plunge on the morning of August 6, 1926, the treacherous water was rough and choppy, so bad that steamboat crossings were canceled. Nevertheless, nineteen-year-old Ederle was determined to make it across. It was a minimum of 21 miles from the French shore to Dover, England—probably longer on this day. She knew she could be tossed off-course by the rough conditions. But not even she could imagine the harrowing challenges that the Channel would present.

She covered her body with olive oil, lanolin, and lard, a mixture designed not only to keep her warm but also to protect her from stinging jellyfish or Portuguese men-of-war. Wearing a daring two-piece black silk suit with a tiny American flag sewn over one breast, a red rubber cap, and amber-glass goggles, Ederle waited impatiently to make the plunge.

Finally, she shouted, "Cheerio," and dived into the cold, dark water. It was a little after seven o'clock in the morning...

☙☙

Whether spending summers as a kid at the family's riverside bungalow in Highlands, New Jersey, or paddling around in the Tenth Avenue horse troughs in Manhattan, Gertrude Ederle had always felt comfortable around water.

Gertrude Ederle

Gertrude grew up as a water baby. One could see the Shrewsbury River from their summer home in New Jersey. "Her father would lower her into the water with a rope around her little waist, and she would paddle about and laugh up at him, entirely unafraid," Gertrude's mother said. As a young girl she was a daredevil; she loved to roam the streets of New York or hitch rides on the back of ice trucks.

The third of six children, Gertrude was inspired by her older sister Margaret, a good swimmer, to take up the sport. After years of swimming together, the two joined the Women's Swimming Association of New York.

Gertrude first grabbed national attention in 1922 at a race in the New York area. A total unknown, she finished the $3\frac{1}{2}$-mile Joseph P. Day Cup at Manhattan Beach ahead of fifty-one other swimmers, including U.S. swimming superstar Helen Wainwright and British champion Hilda James.

Ederle, the bashful, broad-shouldered daughter of a New York butcher, was on her way. She spent the next couple of years destroying just about every woman's swimming record in the books—from the 50 yards to the half-mile. She won more than two dozen trophies and set twenty-nine world and national swimming records. She was rapidly becoming a swimmer of international repute. At the 1924 Olympics in Paris, Ederle added to her reputation by winning a gold medal and two bronzes. The next year she was the first woman to complete the traditional 21-mile race from the docks of New York City to Sandy Hook, New Jersey. She was proud to be the first woman to do it, but prouder still to break the men's record with a time of 7 hours, 11 minutes, and 30 seconds. She liked breaking down stereotypes about women and breaking records, particularly those held by men.

In 1925, the coach of the Women's Swimming Association of New York selected Margaret instead of Gertrude to try to swim the English Channel. But Margaret deferred to her younger sister. She knew that "Gertie," as the family called her, was the faster swimmer.

When Gertrude Ederle announced her intention to swim the English Channel, there was hardly an outcry of public support. Even though many people regarded her as one of the world's great swimmers, they just didn't think a woman could accomplish such a feat. Reported the *London Daily News:* "Even the most uncompromising champion of the rights and capacities of women must admit that in contests of physical skill, speed and endurance, they must remain forever the weaker sex."

The newspaper's prediction seemed to be fulfilled when, after nine hours out, Ederle became seasick and overwhelmed by the treacherous currents. Her trainer, Jabez Wolffe, ordered her to quit. She refused and he had to pull her kicking and screaming from the water. Ederle had lost a chance to reach her goal. And her father, Harry, had lost $5,000, the sum he had bet on his daughter to finish.

The irate swimmer dismissed Wolffe. She made up her mind to come back the next year for a second attempt. She found a new trainer, William Burgess, who had swum across the Channel in 1911 after thirty-two attempts. Gertrude's father promised that this time he would not allow anyone to pull her from the water without her permission.

Gertrude Ederle wasn't the only woman with designs to swim the Channel. Three days before Ederle's attempt, Clarabelle Barrett of New Rochelle, New York, was lost in the fog for an hour or so before giving up 2 miles from the French shore. And Lillian Cannon of Baltimore was also getting ready for the swim.

Ederle's second crack at the Channel drew a bit more attention than the first. By now she had become a symbol of the American ideals of courage, spirit, and determination. She signed a contract to tell her story to newspapers. Hardly a day passed during her training period when the press did not mention her or when her words didn't make headlines. "Trudy," as she had been dubbed by journalists, had become a media darling.

Ederle's father made news himself when he bet $25,000 on his daughter to pull off what many thought to be impossible. That princely sum represented the sale of a lot of hamburgers, hot dogs, and cold cuts at the family butcher shop on Amsterdam Avenue. Harry Ederle stood to gain $175,000 with his long-shot bet with world famous insurance company Lloyd's of London.

Bringing glory to the United States and proving critics wrong about female athletes would have been enough

Ederle becomes the first woman to swim the English Channel in 1926.

motivation for Gertrude, but her father provided another incentive. He promised her a "roadster"—a popular car of the day—if she mastered the Channel.

On that blustery August morning in 1926, the young swimmer was ready. She surveyed the bustling scene at Cape Gris-Nez. Two tugboats were going to follow her on her great adventure. One boat carried her father, her sister Margaret, and her trainer Burgess. The other one was full of reporters and photographers.

"Please, God, help me," Gertrude said under her breath. Then she plunged into the surly water.

Burgess had planned for Ederle to drift on the tide for a

good part of the trip, conserving her energy for four hours of hard swimming at the end. The Channel, however, would not cooperate. The water was turbulent, and the strong crosscurrents pulled Ederle around like a limp rag doll. Because of the rough swell, Ederle nearly quit seven minutes after starting. But she swam on, blithely timing her strokes while singing "Let Me Call You Sweetheart." Finally Burgess told her to stop singing so that she could save her breath.

She needed every lungful. The waves pushed Ederle in every direction, at times out of sight of the tugboats and leaving her with "an eerie feeling" that she was stranded at sea. When the tugboats finally caught up with her, the reporters and photographers tried to keep up Ederle's spirits by reading cables from her mother (some of which they made up) and singing another hit tune of the time, "Yes, We Have No Bananas." There may have been no bananas, but there were plenty of sugar cubes, pineapple juice, chocolate, and chicken legs. To help Gertrude keep up her strength, people on the boat extended food to her on a pole. If she touched the boats, her Channel attempt would be nullified.

In the afternoon, vicious squalls kicked up and rocked the tugboats. The water was so choppy that many aboard became ill. Ederle was sick, too. Burgess begged her to quit.

Not missing a beat, Ederle yelled back over her shoulder, "WHAT FOR?"

Courage, spirit, and determination, indeed.

Her body ached as she fought through gales. But she continued with a fierce, almost inhuman dedication. Chew another sugar block. Eat a piece of chocolate. Down another shot of pineapple juice. "About eight hours out I knew I would either swim it or drown."

Day turned into night. The strong currents swept her off her intended course. But Ederle kept going, and now she could finally make out the bonfires on the English shore. Thousands of people had gathered there, waiting to give her a heroine's welcome.

After swimming more than fourteen hours and many miles out of her way, Ederle was feeling the strain. The final 400 yards were brutal, every stroke an agony and every part of her body aching as she headed toward shore.

At last it was down to the final 50 yards.

Flares filled the night sky and a spotlight illuminated the white foam that Ederle was kicking up behind her. Machine-like, she headed toward the shore's promised land.

At 9:40 P.M., she dragged herself onto land at Kingsdown, a couple of miles north of her intended destination of Dover. Thundering cheers went up for Ederle, although she seemed more dead than alive. She keeled over, doubled up by cramps for an hour—too sick to immediately enjoy her magnificent achievement.

What Ederle had done, though, was past human understanding. Not only had she completed the journey across treacherous, life-threatening waters, but she had also—in spite of going an estimated 14 miles out of her way—broken the world record by a full two hours! Her time: 14 hours, 31 minutes.

Suddenly, America had a new sports hero bigger than life. The newspapers were full of praise for this extraordinary woman. Ederle, with her indefatigable spirit, became a legend in her own time. In at least one 1926 poll, she finished ahead of Babe Ruth as the most popular athlete in America.

If all that acclaim was hard for the modest Ederle to believe, even more unbelievable was the hero's welcome that greeted her in New York on her return. Ederle might have been ready for the Channel swim, but she was certainly not ready for this: two million screaming people lined the route for a riotous ticker-tape parade through the city.

Nor was she ready for the numerous stage and screen offers, swimsuit endorsements, and proposals of marriage that followed. Irving Berlin, one of the most popular songwriters in the U.S., wrote a song—"Trudy"—in her honor.

Wholesome. Unspoiled. Thoroughly natural. That's what they wrote about her in the newspapers. All she had wanted to do was swim the English Channel and prove something to the world, and to herself.

"When somebody tells me I cannot do something," Ederle said, "that's when I do it."

She certainly did.

2
BABE DIDRIKSON ZAHARIAS
The Other Babe

I t's just a publicity stunt. It is difficult and unheard of. But if she succeeds, she will catch the world's attention. The question is: Can Mildred Didrikson pull it off?

Melvin McCombs, her boss at the Employers Casualty Company in Dallas, Texas, believed in her. She couldn't let him down.

In the summer of 1932, hundreds of young women gathered in Evanston, Illinois, for the national AAU track and field championships and Olympic trials.

Didrikson poses with her trophy at the Miami Biltmore Country Club in 1940.

McCombs had come up with a scheme to get publicity for his firm and his star. He had brought Didrikson to the AAU meet as a member of his company's track team—the only member. She was the entire team!

Other teams had as many as twenty or more athletes.

"I'm going to lick you single-handed," Didrikson announced. To her AAU opponents, it sounded ridiculous. The media loved it: One woman against the rest of the country.

This brash young woman was different. Most females of her time weren't outspoken. They accepted their role as the "weaker sex."

But the word "weak" wasn't in her vocabulary. "My goal," she later wrote, "is to be the greatest athlete in the world." Not the greatest female athlete. The greatest athlete!

In two previous AAU championships, Didrikson had made a strong showing. This time the stakes were higher: a place on the U.S. track team at the Olympics.

At the AAU meet Didrikson entered as many events as was humanly possible. In less than three hours, she raced around the University of Illinois's Dyche Stadium. She competed in both the qualifying heats and finals of each event.

Finish one event, race to the next. At each stop, the officials gave her a few seconds to catch her breath. Then, she was up and running again.

How would this one-woman team measure up?

By the time the meet was over, Didrikson had finished first in five events: the broad jump, 80-meter hurdles, javelin toss, baseball toss, and shot put. She set world records in three of them. And she tied for first in the high jump, giving her more points by herself than any other team in the entire event.

Her total of thirty points had beaten everyone. Her score was eight points better than the runner-up, the Illinois Women's Athletic Club, a squad with twenty-two athletes!

What a one-woman show. What a headline for the newspapers. Gushed the *New York Times:* "The most amazing series of performances ever accomplished by an individual, male or female, in track and field history." She had conquered the best in the United States. Now she was ready to conquer the world.

The meet in Evanston was the start of an unmatched career in athletics. How did it all begin?

Mildred Ella Didriksen's—later changed to Didrikson—parents had come to America from Norway, hoping to find a better life for their family. Soon after they arrived, America slipped into the Great Depression that followed the stock market crash of 1929. Mildred's father, a former cabinet-maker, earned a meager living by refinishing furniture. Her mother took in washing and ironing from the neighbors.

The family was poor. Everyone had to help bring in income. That included Mildred. As a young girl, she picked figs for farmers and did odd jobs for the neighbors.

But even though times were tough, Mildred always found ways to make life fun. When she went to the store, she didn't walk, she ran. She wanted to see how fast she could go. Each day she would try to go faster and faster. She was delighted when she shaved seconds off her run.

Mildred loved to leap over the neighbors' hedges. To make the jumps easier, she asked her neighbors to trim their hedges to the same height, and they were kind enough to oblige. It was better, but some of the bushes were prickly. When Mildred jumped, she tried crooking one leg and extending it higher to avoid being scratched. Her new technique worked. Now she leaped over one hedge after another, hurtling forward, trying to best her time on her way to school.

Later, Mildred would object when people called her a "natural" athlete. There was nothing natural about the hard work she put in to master her skills.

The Didriksen family philosophy was to work hard, play hard.

Mildred's father was a physical fitness fanatic. He built gymnasium equipment for his family and installed it in the backyard of their home in Beaumont, Texas. And he expected the whole family to work out. All the neighborhood kids were attracted to the Didriksens' backyard. At the time Mildred was growing up, girls didn't usually compete against boys. But with four brothers in her own family, she soon learned to compete against them and the neighborhood boys in a variety of sports.

At some point Mildred became known as "Babe." Some say it was because as the sixth of seven children she was the baby of the family; others say it was because she could hit a baseball like Babe Ruth. That explanation seems reasonable: she once hit five home runs in a game.

Babe's athletic talent in high school was apparent from the start. It set her apart from the other students. The boys teased her. Never one to be intimidated, she beat them up when the teasing got too rough. The girls kept her out of their groups. Who wanted to pal around with someone who competed with the boys? Who wanted to be friends with someone who bragged that one day she would be "the greatest athlete that ever lived"?

Her classmates might not have wanted her in their groups at first, but they soon learned to love her on the field. Babe became one of the most popular and respected girls at Beaumont Senior High School. She starred in every girls' sport that was available: basketball, tennis, golf, swimming, and diving.

She was still a high school student when Employers Casualty Company of Dallas came calling. Would she like to join the insurance company and play with the Golden Cyclones? They were one of the nation's top women's amateur basketball teams. Babe was excited. She moved to Dallas with her father's blessing. She went to work as a typist at the insurance company. Her salary of $900 was considered overly generous for the times. But she had no illusions—she knew she had been hired mostly for her athletic ability, not her typing skills.

Babe was an office worker by day, a sports star in her off

time. Her school made special arrangements for her to take final exams and graduate with her high school class. In the meantime, she played sports to her heart's content—basketball, softball, tennis, and swimming. It was in track and field, though, that she really excelled. She competed on the Golden Cyclones' track and field team and participated in three national AAU (Amateur Athletic Union) championships.

Her goal was the Olympics. After her astounding performance at the 1932 Olympic trials in Evanston, she was well on her way to her goal—and she had the nation's attention.

Babe had qualified to compete in five events at the '32 Games. But she was only allowed to enter three. Officials had eliminated the 800-meter run for women from the Olympics. Many people thought such a long race was too hard for women. They believed that women were more fragile than men, not only physically but also mentally. Concluded one national health organization: "Under prolonged and intense strain a girl goes to pieces nervously."

Babe was about to prove otherwise. She brought a cocky attitude to the Los Angeles Olympics. A teammate started to brag about how well she had done. Babe cast a stone-cold glare in her direction. "Oh, I done that, and in half the time."

The outspoken Didrikson was not the most popular athlete on the American squad. When it came time to choose a captain for Team USA, her teammates voted for Jean Shiley. Babe knew Shiley only too well. She had tied Babe in a closely fought high-jump competition at the 1932 AAU meet prior to the Olympics.

The first Olympic event for Babe was the javelin throw. As she unleashed the throw, she felt a twinge in her right shoulder. The javelin landed 143 feet, 4 inches away. Her throw was a world record, shattering the previous record by nearly 11 feet. She had torn cartilage in her shoulder, but won the Olympic title.

Then Babe got ready for the 80-meter hurdle. She had no trouble jumping while racing at full speed. She had perfected her distinct style when leaping over the neighborhood hedges during her childhood days. Now instead of hedges, it was hurdles.

Babe broke the world record in the 80-meter hurdle on her first try. But—hold on—officials announced that she had jumped the gun. She would have to run it over again.

Once again, Babe was off. Once more, she was called back for starting before the gun went off.

On her third try, Babe again pushed off her mark. This time, she wasn't ahead of the gun. She broke her own world record—the one that she had set just moments before—by racing the 80-meter distance in 11.7 seconds. The result stood. Babe claimed her second gold medal of the Olympics.

Next up, the high jump.

Babe faced her rival Jean Shiley for the gold medal. The two athletes presented a dramatic contrast in styles. Didrikson used the so-called "western roll," throwing herself over the bar headfirst. She called it her "men's style." Shiley used the scissor-kick style, going over the bar feet first. It was the classic high-jump technique for women of that day.

Both women cleared the bar at a world record 5 feet, 5 $1/4$ inches. They had tied again.

The judges met. The decision? They declared Shiley the gold medal winner. They said Babe "dove" over the bar, her head clearing before her body. This technique was not allowed in those days. Using it barred Babe from sharing the gold medal. (She was ahead of her time. In later years, the "western roll" would become the style for all high jumpers.) She was disappointed. She had to settle for second place and the silver. But Babe had medalled in every event she had entered. Her total was now one silver and two gold.

Along with her medals came a barrage of publicity. Flashbulbs popped. Cameras moved in for close-ups of America's newest sports darling. One photo showed Babe posing with Hollywood's handsome leading man, Clark Gable. And Babe loved the attention.

Three Olympic medals in three tries. How was Babe going to top that?

How about playing professional baseball and basketball with men? Touring the country giving billiards and boxing exhibitions? Competing on foot against a racehorse? Doing a vaudeville act? There seemed to be no end to Babe's diverse talents.

Colorful and full of ego, Babe enjoyed boasting that she

could do anything. The media loved it. The audience ate it up. She was the ultimate show-woman and a shameless self-promoter.

Her barnstorming tours made money, plenty of it. She earned as much as $55,000 a year—a staggering amount during the Depression years. She was able to support her parents, send her nieces and nephews through school, and ensure her own future.

When Babe looked to her future, she had visions of being a champion in golf. Why golf? "I'd done everything else," she said.

Skeptics pointed out one problem. She had no golfing experience. A lack of experience might have been a problem for most anyone else, but not for Babe. As she had in other sports, Babe attacked golf with passion.

She practiced six days a week. At times her caddie would stand 150 yards away with an empty golf bag. Babe would chip the golf ball into the bag over and over again. "If the caddie had to move it, she got mad," said Babe's nephew, Dee Didriksen. "I remember her hands would be calloused, and they would bleed..."

Babe's size—a trim 5-foot-7 and 145 pounds—was perfect for golf. She displayed enormous power with her swing. The press referred to her as a "muscle woman." She hated the nickname, yet it was appropriate: she had the strength to outdistance some of the greatest players in the world.

Asked how she did it, the green-eyed Babe usually

responded with a wink, "I just lift up my girdle and let it fly!"

She was soon winning women's amateur tournaments around the country. And putting on exhibitions with stars from the men's game.

Babe would stroll down the green. While other golfers ignored the fans, Babe would stop and chat. She would make wisecracks and joke with them.

"She loved people and people loved her," said women's golfing great Patty Berg.

Not everybody on the golf circuit found her lovable, though. The genteel game of golf had never seen the likes of Babe. She was trash-talking long before it was popular among athletes.

In one pro-am tournament, Babe was paired with golfing great Sam Snead. She stepped up to the tee and hit a long drive. "See if you can beat that poke, Sam," she taunted.

He couldn't.

She was just as hard on the women.

The brash, self-confident Babe would enter the clubhouse and inquire, "Which one of you is finishing second this week?"

It was not surprising that she would try competing with the men at their own game. Babe merely filled out an application and entered the 1938 Los Angeles Open. The operators of the PGA event were thrilled. The tournament had been struggling. It wouldn't hurt to have a celebrity like Babe on the course.

Babe Didrikson Zaharias

Didrikson chips out of a sand trap during a 1947 women's golf tournament in Miami.

As a publicity stunt, the organizers paired Babe with a minister and a former pro wrestler nicknamed "The Crying Greek from Cripple Creek." His name: George Zaharias.

As expected, this odd trio drew the biggest crowds of the tournament. Something happened, though, that was completely unexpected. Romance bloomed on a golf course. Babe and George fell in love. They married later that year.

While Babe's score failed to qualify at that PGA event, it didn't stop her from trying again. In 1944, she failed once more to make the cut. Then in 1945, she finally succeeded! Babe didn't win the tournament, but she made a good showing against some of the best male golfers in the world. And she had broken the gender barrier. She was the first woman to play on the PGA Tour. Here was a great story. But hardly anyone knew about it at the time.

"There was no TV and if you did radio you had to drive to the station," said golf legend Byron Nelson. No cameras followed the Babe around the course. Fast forward to 2003. Think of the publicity Annika Sorenstam, star of the Ladies Professional Golf Association (LPGA), generated. Her bid to play in a men's tournament was shown on TV all over the world.

Actually, without Babe there might not have been an LPGA. Babe wanted to turn pro. But there was no place for her to go. Instead of giving up, she helped to found the Ladies Professional Golf Association in 1947. She became its immediate star, bringing women's golf to the forefront in America.

Babe played in tournaments and tirelessly promoted the sport. She appeared in hundreds of exhibitions. She always had a story or two to tell the press, some of them even true.

She occasionally stretched the truth to make her stories more colorful. Like the tale about outrunning a locomotive, or the one about racing a wild bull.

According to one story, Babe was caught red-handed telling a fib. On a fishing trip during the Second World War, she was asked, for security purposes, to give her date of birth.

Babe Didrikson Zaharias

"Nineteen-nineteen," she said.

"So you were thirteen when you won those Olympic medals, huh, Babe?" said a friend.

Babe smirked.

"Aw, shaddup," she said.

Winning tournament after tournament on the women's tour, Babe was on top of the world. But in 1953, she faced the toughest opponent of her life: cancer. She underwent surgery. About three months later, she was back on the tour and winning once more.

In 1954, despite the spread of the cancer, she racked up five more tour victories. It was her last stand in the spotlight.

On September 27, 1956, Babe died. An entire nation mourned.

She had left an amazing legacy.

The Associated Press named her the greatest female athlete of the twentieth century. Babe tried almost every sport—and very often dominated it. And she did so in a time when women were not supposed to exert themselves in sports. A Hall of Famer in not one, but two sports—in track and field and in golf—Babe destroyed all the "weaker sex" stereotypes. She proved it was okay for women to sweat, grunt, and groan in the athletic arena.

"She brought it to the forefront that women could be athletes, too," said former golfing great Marlene Hagge.

And no one did it better than Babe.

3
SUSAN BUTCHER
The Magnificent Musher

Susan Butcher was making plans for her survival.

Ax, check. Snowshoes and sleeping bag, check.

Enough food and water for the long journey.

And the most important, her dogs: Siberian huskies, powerful allies on the most treacherous trail of all.

Everything was in order. She was ready to start the 1990

Susan Butcher with her dogs in March, 1987

Iditarod Trail Sled Dog Race. Sometimes called the "Last Great Race on Earth," this grueling course was a huge challenge for both man and beast. She was gunning for her fourth Iditarod title.

She grabbed the handlebar and looked over her sixteen dogs. Their bodies were tense, straining, ready to go.

Butcher, clad in a bright red snowsuit, was eager to get started, too. Not that she liked the conditions. The heaviest snowstorm in twenty-five years had hit the area, followed by unseasonably warm weather. A part of the 1,168-mile trail through the daunting Alaskan wilderness had turned to slush.

The weather was not the only concern. Dangerous trail conditions and wild animals could also jeopardize her journey.

Memories of the nightmarish 1985 Iditarod were always with her. After finishing in the top five in several earlier races, Butcher was breezing along on her way to victory. Everything had been going well. Suddenly, without warning, a huge moose appeared on the trail. Wild and out of control, it was headed directly toward her sled!

Before Butcher could react, the crazed animal had attacked the huskies. The harnessed dogs were attached to each other and the sled. They hadn't had a chance against a six-foot-tall, 1,500-pound wild beast. The raging moose went on a rampage. There was blood everywhere in the snow.

Butcher, not thinking of her own safety, had grabbed her ax. She'd struck the moose again and again in an effort to stop the massacre. Suddenly, a shot had rung out. Another dog-sled driver, seeing her peril, had shot and killed the attacker.

But the damage had been done: two dogs dead and thirteen injured. There was no question she was out of the race. Libby Riddles went on to become the first woman to win the Iditarod. But Butcher couldn't worry about having to drop out of the Last Great Race. Her dogs were not out of danger. Grieving, she had traveled with her wounded dogs to a veterinary hospital. She'd slept on the hospital floor for a week. Despite suffering with an injured shoulder, she'd cared for her dogs until they were healthy enough to go home.

Butcher tried to shake the terrible images from her mind. She was determined to finish the race first again. Could she become the first woman to win the Iditarod four times?

❧❧

Susan Butcher had always seemed to be more comfortable with animals than she was with people.

When she was just a little girl growing up in Cambridge, Massachusetts, she hated the city. But she loved the great outdoors. She loved spending time at her family's summer home on the rocky Maine coast. She especially enjoyed restoring a boat with her father and sister, Kate. It was hard work, but it was worth it. Sailing was such fun. Susan never wanted to be in the city again!

And she loved animals—all kinds. Susan's mother came to expect the unexpected—she wasn't even surprised the time she came home and found iguanas crawling up her curtains.

One day Susan received a present: a Siberian husky. The teenager was so excited she went to the library to learn more about huskies. She discovered they are bred to be sled dogs. A year later, she bought another, at which point her mom suggested the house wasn't big enough for both dogs.

Susan, who was always independent, went to live with her grandmother in Maine.

After high school she headed west to Colorado with dreams of raising dogs and living in the great outdoors. There were few places in America more wide open and wild than the Colorado Rockies.

Working with a veterinarian in Boulder, she became skilled in treating animals. Handling dogs was second nature to Susan. A local woman gave her a chance. Soon Susan was training and raising sled dogs. She loved to take them out on training runs, but she was unhappy with the lack of sled dog trails in the area.

"I had to go in a truck to get to trails," she said.

One day in 1975, Susan was reading a magazine about mushers, the people who race sled dogs. An article about a sled dog race in Alaska called the Iditarod caught her eye. She was intrigued. Alaska! At last she had discovered a place where there were thousands of miles of trails.

She made up her mind that she was going to compete in the Iditarod.

The race was named after a trail that mushers took in the early 1900s to bring mail and supplies to Alaskan mining towns. The Iditarod began each year in March in Anchorage—dashing across the Alaskan range, turning west along the Yukon River, and zooming north along the Bering Sea coast into Nome. It took about two weeks to complete. With its frozen rivers, rough mountain ranges, bleak terrain, windswept coast, and often subzero temperatures, it was no place for the weakhearted. But Butcher was determined to go.

Four months after arriving in Fairbanks, Alaska, the twenty-one-year-old made plans to prepare for the Iditarod. She bought three pedigree dogs. She loaded them into a truck along with her two cats and food supplies and headed off into the rugged Wrangell Mountains.

She settled in a small log cabin built in the Gold Rush years of the early 1900s. There wasn't another human being around for forty miles. Living in the mountains was hard. The only water available was in a nearby stream. Butcher lugged buckets and buckets of water from the stream to her cabin. For heat, she chopped wood. She hunted and trapped moose, caribou, and sheep for food. It was not an easy life, but Butcher was happy. She was able to mush her dogs on the plentiful trails. She rarely saw another person until the summer, when she went into Fairbanks to earn enough money to buy supplies for the next winter.

Butcher signed on for the summer to help with a University of Alaska project to save the endangered musk oxen and earned $600.

Although Butcher was happy with her new life, it was still her dream to race in the Iditarod. Some people considered the Last Great Race a "no-woman's land." Women had run the race, but no woman had ever won. Men usually had an advantage when it came to moving the heavy sled up and down tricky slopes and around trees. When loaded with supplies and equipment, the sleds weighed hundreds of pounds. Mushers needed strong legs to run behind the sleds and push on the uphill stretches.

Butcher was not concerned. Even though she stood only 5-foot-6 and weighed 140 pounds, she was wiry and strong. She felt she could outwork any man.

In 1977, Butcher met Joe Redington Sr., one of the founders of the Iditarod. Redington agreed that she was fit to compete, especially after watching her work in his kennel. Butcher needed two huskies to complete her team. They made a deal: she would train young dogs for Redington in exchange for the two huskies.

Now Butcher needed a company or corporation to back her. It is expensive to enter the Iditarod, and Butcher was broke. She tried to get sponsors herself by going door to door, but wasn't able to raise much money.

Redington came up with a plan to get Butcher in the news. Local television viewers were surprised by what they saw on their screens. There on a frozen lake, Susan Butcher stood with an ax in her hand. In the freezing temperatures, she wore only a bathing suit. After chopping a hole in the ice, she jumped in and emerged smiling. "And this is how a future Iditarod competitor keeps clean," the reporter announced.

The plan worked. The publicity helped Butcher get her first sponsor. In 1978 she entered the race. She became the first woman to finish in the top twenty and in the money.

Susan Butcher

Four years earlier, Mary Shields and Lolly Medley, the first women to compete in the Ititarod, had finished out of the money, eight days behind the winner.

Even though Butcher had finished among the money winners, she was not satisfied.

For three years, she kept improving.

"There are many hard things in life," Butcher said, "but there's only one sad thing, and that is giving up."

She didn't give up. She entered the 1982 race. The race was only one hour old when Butcher ran into trouble. Her sled careened off course and plowed into a tree. The crack-up left Butcher bruised. She checked her fifteen dogs. Four were injured.

Further down the trail Butcher and her team drove into a blinding snowstorm. It was difficult enough to drive against the wind and snow, but now the orange markers set alongside the trail as guides were invisible.

Suddenly, Butcher found herself 10 miles off course. She managed to fight her way back. She reached one of the twenty-four checkpoints on the course where drivers store additional food and equipment. There they can stop and rest or take care of injured or sick dogs. Iditarod drivers are required to take a 24-hour break during the race. But Butcher was forced into a 52-hour stay. A vicious snowstorm stranded her at Shaktoolik, the first checkpoint on the Bering coast.

During the unexpected delay, her first priority was the dogs. She knew the routine: melt down snow for water, feed the dogs, check them over, fix the harnesses. In addition,

Butcher had to chop wood in the face of 80-mile-per-hour winds and 30-foot snowdrifts. She barely had time to catch a little sleep. Despite all this difficulty, she managed to finish in second place.

In the 1984 Iditarod, more trouble. Butcher was racing along a frozen Norton Sound Bay when she heard a frightening noise. The ice was cracking! Suddenly, Butcher and her sled plunged into the dark, freezing water.

Granite, the lead dog, took charge. He pulled with all his might. The other dogs grunted and strained. They struggled to gain a foothold on the slippery surface. Finally, they pulled Butcher out of the water. Her dogs had saved her life! Soaking wet and chilled to the bone, she ran behind the sled for several miles to stay warm. Amazingly, she once again finished second.

The next year, the raging moose spoiled Butcher's plans to become the first woman to win the Iditarod. Having to drop out of the race was bad enough. But sitting by while Libby Riddles became the first female to win the Iditarod made Butcher feel even worse.

"It hurt when Libby won," Butcher said. "But there's more to it than that. I didn't get to race the team I had been working on for seven years. That's what hurt."

Finally, success. She won the 1986 Iditarod in record time. After winning in 1987 and 1988, she became the first person to win the event three straight years.

Butcher won other races, but enjoyed the challenge of the Iditarod most of all.

Susan Butcher

*Susan Butcher nears the finish line of the
1990 Iditarod Sled Dog Race.*

She missed winning the championship in 1989. Now it was 1990 and Butcher hoped to reclaim her title.

"All right! Go!" she shouted and squeezed the handlebar. Her powerful team of sixteen dogs was off and running into the Alaskan wilderness.

Because there were seventy mushers, the starting times for the race were staggered. Butcher started as No. 68. But by the time she reached Shaktoolik, she was in the lead. It was close, though. The first three mushers pulled into the area within just eight minutes of each other.

During the race, it is not unusual for dogs to get sick or injured and have to drop out. But suddenly, Butcher had to replace three—including two important lead dogs. One of them was Tolstoy, her favorite. Butcher alternated taking the lead with Lavon Barve and defending champion Joe Runyan.

Butcher had not slept much during the race. Drowsiness and exhaustion are major problems for Iditarod mushers. To wake herself up, she liked to scoop up a handful of snow and throw it in her face.

Her fatigue caused her to imagine things at times. "I'd think I was seeing Tolstoy in the lead," she said.

No, Tolstoy was no longer there, but Lightning and Sluggo, the two new lead dogs, were doing just fine. Butcher took the lead again as she headed along the windswept Bering Sea coastal area—the home stretch—with 270 miles to go.

Butcher's dogs were familiar with the area. She had often brought them there to practice in the wet and windy conditions.

"They know where White Mountain is," said Butcher, referring to the last checkpoint before the final 77 miles into Nome.

Susan Butcher

For the dogs, it was like going home. By the time Butcher's sled reached White Mountain, she was comfortably in front of her closest competitor.

They still had to complete the treacherous crossing of Norton Sound Bay at night. It was 30 miles of sheer ice, and Butcher had not forgotten the experience of 1984 when she almost drowned.

This time, no problem.

As she approached the outskirts of Nome on a bone-chilling, zero-degree day, the word spread around town. The fire siren sounded to alert the townspeople: First musher in!

Students were dismissed from school and ran into the streets in celebration. People emptied out of stores and rushed to Front Street. They didn't seem to notice the frigid temperature. The crowds couldn't wait to get a glimpse of the Iditarod winner. Shouts of congratulations filled the air when they spotted Susan Butcher in her red snowsuit.

Butcher finished the last few yards running alongside her dogs. Once the sled had stopped, she hugged her two lead dogs. Then she embraced her husband, John Monson, a lawyer and fellow musher, who was waiting for her at the finish line. He helped train the dogs and run a kennel near their home in the tiny wilderness town of Eureka, Alaska. In racking up her fourth Iditarod title in five years, she didn't just win—she won with surprising ease. She came in hours ahead of the runner-up.

"This team had power coming out of its ears," Butcher

said with a tired smile. Ice was caked to her eyelashes. She had finished the race in a record 11 days, 1 hour, 53 minutes, and 20 seconds.

Seven of the seventy starters had dropped out. Another was disqualified. Most of the mushers were strung out some 600 miles behind Butcher. They would be hobbling into Nome at various times for at least another week.

For many years dog-sled racing was thought to be strictly a man's domain because of its harsh, unyielding conditions. That is, until Butcher shattered the myth. She showed she was as good as any man running a dog-sled race—in fact, better than most.

Her success sparked the phrase: "Alaska—where men are men and women win the Iditarod."

4

JULIE KRONE
The Horse Whisperer

It was the last day of the 1993 summer racing season at Saratoga Race Track. Julie Krone climbed aboard her mount, Seattle Way.

One more victory. That's all she needed for the riding championship. The 4-foot-10, 100-pound jockey settled in the saddle, gripped the reins, and squeezed the whip in her right hand.

There had been countless other starts for the thirty-year-old Krone. She was the most successful female jockey in thoroughbred horse racing history. But although she had competed in some 16,000 races, every new start was as

Krone rests for a moment at Monmouth Park Racetrack in 1990.

fresh as the first time. Racing was her passion. It was the only thing she had ever wanted to do.

It explained why she had always bounced back from frightful injuries. There had been enough of those to discourage any rider.

Krone stayed deep in the saddle, waiting for the start of the Saratoga race. The sun splashed on Krone's brightly colored riding gear. The track was dry and the skies were blue—a beautiful day for a race at the historic upstate New York track.

The gates slammed open. They're off!

Twelve sleek, muscular horses shot out of the starting gate and around the track. Krone battled for position with her fellow jockeys. Her face was grim, streaked with sweat and dirt.

Krone stayed behind the leaders for most of the race, pacing her horse. With the race heading into the last turn, Krone found herself behind a wall of thundering thousand-pound animals. The crowd was on its feet, screaming.

As she had done so many times before, Krone was about to make her move for the homestretch run. She tightened her hold on the reins. Suddenly, the jockey on her left steered his horse into her path.

"No! No!" Krone screamed as she stood up in the saddle.

Too late.

The horses collided. Seattle Way buckled, throwing Krone out of the saddle. She flew head over foot and landed hard on her right ankle.

The video replay was scary. As one sports writer described it, Krone looked like "a brightly colored rag doll flopping crazily onto the turf."

Julie Krone

She had completely spun over and was sitting on the turf facing back down the track. A horse was heading straight for her! She was unable to move.

"I knew he was going to hit me."

The jockey, Jorge Chavez, tried desperately to steer Two Is Trouble out of Krone's way. The horse was going too fast. His hooves hit hard, striking her in the chest and elbow. Her body did another tumble.

She lay there, not moving. As he looked back, Chavez thought, "Oh, no…"

Krone was barely alive when taken to the hospital. A special protective vest that covered her heart had saved her!

She underwent several operations.

Friends came in to try to cheer her. Fellow jockeys visited, too. Fans wrote letters. But when she went home to rehab at her Jockey Hollow Farm, she was depressed and scared. Scared she could be permanently injured. Scared she would never race again.

⊙⊚

Horseback riding came naturally to Julie Krone. She was in the saddle before she learned to walk. Her mother Judi, an equestrian champion, saw to that. "Even before I knew I'd be a jockey, my mom helped prepare me for the work," Julie said.

But she had to grow up first. She lived on a horse farm in Eau Claire, Michigan. Admittedly a "wild kid," she loved the thrill of racing horses. The faster the better.

"If something was dangerous, I didn't care," Krone said. "I valued the thrill a lot more than I valued myself."

LADIES FIRST

Tiny Julie raced horses around the family farm with reckless abandon. She loved performing tricks, even though they were dangerous. With her horse at top speed, Julie stood straight up in the saddle. She jumped fences holding the reins in her mouth!

"It was like going to a rocket launch every day," said Krone's father, Don, an art teacher. "She was always on her pony. She always had some trick to show you. She was fearless."

One day her father found Julie high up in a tree.

"Better look out. You'll fall."

"I already did," Julie answered. "Watch me climb."

Danger was a part of Julie Krone's life. She loved every minute of it.

"I got bit, I got stepped on, I got kicked in the head," Krone recalled. "I got dumped five miles from home; the pony ran back and I had to walk."

Julie was still very much like a young colt herself, still trying to find her legs. When it came to Julie's education with horses, her mother always managed to be around.

Julie loved to compete in horse shows. Her specialty: dressage, the art of training a horse in obedience. When she entered a horse show, she fully expected to win. One year she entered the 21-and-under division at a county fair. She took home the blue ribbon for first place. She was only five years old!

By the time she was a teenager, Julie had already decided

on her future. She and her mother watched the Belmont Stakes on TV when Steve Cauthen was going for the Triple Crown aboard Affirmed. As Cauthen raced across the finish line ahead of the field, Julie turned to her mother and said, "I want to be a jockey." She was fourteen.

One year later, Julie and her mom, now divorced, were on their way to Kentucky. Judi Krone's connections had turned up a job for both of them—walking racehorses around the famous Churchill Downs track.

Julie's experience at Churchill Downs just confirmed what she already knew: Nothing was going to stop her from being a jockey!

Back in Michigan, she hung around fairground tracks and did some riding. Next stop: Tampa, Florida, to live with her grandparents and ride horses.

But when Julie showed up at the front gate at Tampa Bay Downs racetrack, the guards turned her away. They couldn't believe this little girl was old enough to work at the track.

What did she do? She simply went around the back and climbed a fence. She met one of the track's trainers. He liked Julie's spunk and put her on a horse. In just five weeks, Julie won her first race as a professional.

Krone struck up a friendship with Julie Snellings, a former jockey who had been paralyzed in a race.

One day the jockeys gasped as Krone walked out for a race. Krone was not only wearing Snellings's old riding boots and pants. She was actually wearing her colors, too!

Krone rides to a win in the 2003 Breeders Cup race.

Like other jockeys, they were very superstitious. They felt sure that bad luck would follow.

"I'm real superstitious, too," Snellings said, "and it scared me to death that something might happen to her."

"It was no big deal," Krone said of wearing her friend's colors. "I just wanted to change her luck."

Snellings's colors brought Krone good fortune. For the first time in her budding career, she won three straight races.

It was a good start for Krone. But she had bigger plans, much bigger. Tampa Bay Downs was considered minor league when compared to the major tracks up north. She moved to Baltimore. There she could race at the top Maryland tracks like Pimlico, Laurel, and Bowie.

Julie Krone

When she first started, Julie's agent had problems finding mounts for her. Horse owners didn't think that women were strong enough to handle a 1,000-pound thoroughbred.

"Go home, have babies, do the dishes." The fans' voices echoed in her mind. Even though women had been racing horses professionally since 1968, they were still not generally accepted in the male-dominated racing game.

But now Julie was winning—and slowly being accepted. "She was green, but you could see that horses would run for her," said Bud Delp, a top trainer. "She was a natural."

Delp noticed that Krone had a special way with horses.

"She talks to them, she sings to them. She moves her little fingers on their necks and they just run (hard) for her."

And then, just as Julie's career was getting started, it seemed to come to an abrupt halt.

At Laurel she was thrown from a horse. A broken back. Somehow, she found her way back to the track. Finding the winner's circle was another matter.

Julie hit a slump—eighty straight races without a victory. One day on the backstretch, Julie yelled, "I quit! I quit! I quit! I can't stand it!"

Finally, her luck changed again. Working with Delp, she began winning at Pimlico, Delaware Park, and Atlantic City.

But it took some time for Julie to win the approval of the other jockeys. "The guy riders hated her," Snellings said. "They're used to intimidating the girl riders, and here they were getting intimidated by this little girl." Male jockeys eventually learned to respect Krone, and not only for her skill as a rider. She was a battler, too.

She looked so small, sweet, and innocent—but, boy, could Julie pack a punch!

One day during the final moments of a race at Monmouth Park, Julie was heading into the stretch drive. She and Miguel Rujano were neck and neck in a torrid race. Suddenly, Rujano slashed Krone across the face with his whip.

When the race ended, Krone swung out of the saddle, walked over to Rujano, and punched him in the nose. It started a fight that ended when Krone smashed Rujano with a lawn chair.

This was not the only such incident involving Krone and the other jockeys. "Hey, this is a rough game," she said in her familiar high-pitched, squeaky voice, "and you can't let yourself be a victim out on the track."

Soon she would be toasted with champagne. In 1988 Krone became the leading female jockey in history when she rode her 1,205th winner.

By 1993, Julie could boast a long list of riding titles at many of the country's top tracks. She guided Colonial Affair to victory at Aqueduct's Belmont Stakes. It was part of the Triple Crown, the most elusive title in racing. To gain the Triple Crown, a horse has to win the Kentucky Derby, the Preakness in Maryland, and the Belmont Stakes in New York, all in the same year.

Julie was on top of the world in 1993, enjoying one of her

greatest years on the track—until she came crashing down at Saratoga.

The pain of her injuries eventually went away. Julie's thirst for racing did not. In nine months, she felt well enough to test herself on a horse again. She took quiet rides around the family farm. It was nothing like riding a thoroughbred in a high stakes race, but it was a start. One day on a riding vacation, she took a spill. It was her first fall since the Saratoga race. She got up and brushed herself off. She was fine.

"It was good for me mentally," she said, "I was kind of glad to get that fall out of the way. At that point, I knew I was ready to ride thoroughbreds."

Julie was still scared to go back to racing. But it was her great love. Not going back would have been scarier. For five weeks she prepared for her comeback—working and exercising horses. On May 25, 1994, just nine months since her horrific fall at Saratoga, she ran her first race.

Julie didn't win. But she did finish in the money, in third place.

The next day, Julie hopped aboard a horse named Consider the Lily. It was the sixth race of the day at Belmont, a track she knew only too well.

Her horse pounded out of the starting gate and took the lead. Too soon. Julie pulled on the reins. Consider the Lily dropped behind the leaders. She liked to pace her horse—saving energy for the stretch run.

Finally, with 360 yards to go for the wire, Julie was in second place. Time to make her move.

She pushed Consider the Lily. She pulled alongside a tiring Hayley's Abby. She edged in front.

Waving the Flag came up to challenge. Julie pulled away. She booted Consider the Lily home a length and a half ahead of Waving the Flag.

Victory!

Julie hopped off her horse and headed for the winner's circle. She pumped her right hand in the air as admiring shouts from the stands filled her ears. It was far different than the insulting shouts she had once heard.

"Way to go, Julie!"

"Julie, you're back!"

Then she sprinted through the tunnels toward the jockeys' rooms.

It was just another breakthrough for Krone. Not that she paid much attention to her role as a trailblazer. She merely saw herself as just another jockey.

But her numbers measured up to anyone's. Julie was the first female to win a Triple Crown race. When she retired for the first time in 1999, she had ridden more than 20,000 mounts, won more than 3,500 races, and earned more than $80 million in prize money. Those achievements propelled her right into the Thoroughbred Racing Hall of Fame, a first for a female.

Julie would make other comebacks from terrible spills. She would also come back after her retirement.

Why not? If there was a race to be run, Julie Krone wanted to be there.

5
SHIRLEY MULDOWNEY
Driving Into History

Shirley Muldowney in the driver's seat

*S*hirley Muldowney straps herself into the 8,000-pound Top Fuel dragster that will hurtle her down an asphalt track at more than 300 miles an hour. It is just another day at the track for Muldowney: Drive as fast as possible for one-quarter mile. Fastest car to the finish line wins. Those are the rules of drag racing.

She sits in her dragster, waiting for the race to begin. But is it really Shirley? One really can't tell. The body inside is wrapped from head to toe in a thick, fire-retardant material, topped by a pink helmet. Other than the sponsor's name, all one can see are the eyes peering out.

She's off!

LADIES FIRST

The earth shakes. The grandstands tremble. The noise is deafening, painful to the ears. Then the dragster is off in a cloud of eye-stinging, billowing white smoke. The tires spew black rubber specks like rain from the heavens. The sudden and powerful acceleration sends a vibration through the body, both thrilling and exciting. It is exactly what Shirley Muldowney expects and loves.

It is over in a matter of seconds. By the time the speeding projectile reaches the finish line a quarter-mile away, it needs a parachute to stop. The 24-foot dragster that just moments before was very nearly flying shudders to a halt.

V-r-oom!

Shirley Roque put her foot on the gas pedal as the speedometer climbed higher and higher. The noise shook the quiet neighborhoods of Schenectady, New York. The sleek red Corvette with the daredevil petite fifteen-year-old at the wheel roared down Highway 5 at 120 miles an hour.

Suddenly a police siren shattered the summer night air. Roque pulled over to the side of the road.

As it had many times before, the conversation went something like this:

Shirley: Good evening, Officer Barbieri.
Officer: So it's you again. License and registration, please. (A pause.) It's a dangerous game you're playing, young lady.

But the danger was part of the thrill. Shirley had kept her racing adventures a secret from her parents, too afraid they'd make her quit. She'd sneak out of her bedroom window after her parents had gone to bed, then climb into her souped-up car for another night of drag racing.

Growing up, Shirley had the same problems as most kids. She went to a tough school where she was the target for school bullies. One day she came home from school bruised and battered. She admitted to her father it wasn't the first time. Her father, who had boxed under the name of "Tex Rock," gave her some advice: fight back any way you can.

Shirley never had any problem with school bullies again. By the time she grew up, she had learned never to back down from a challenge of any kind.

"The man gave me the backbone that I needed to survive," she said of her father.

Shirley was not a model student. She cut classes in high school. She didn't hesitate to climb out of a classroom window when the teacher wasn't looking. She often left school and dashed down the street to meet her boyfriend, Jack Muldowney. He's the one who introduced her to speed racing.

"I used to work in a little car-hop restaurant," she said. "Jack Muldowney used to give me a ride home, which was about a mile from the place. But we always took the long route so we could pick up some street races to and from."

It wasn't long before Shirley was racing Jack's car, challenging other hot-rodders. By 1956, when she turned sixteen, she had a learner's permit and a marriage license. Shirley Roque was now Shirley Muldowney.

"Her husband liked to go fast and he built her a car to go a little faster," remembered Shirley's mother, Mae Roque. "It all ended up faster and faster."

Shirley bought her first car for $40. It was a 1940 Ford coupe.

"Jack put a Cadillac engine in it for me," she said. "Guys heard about this and they would come from Amsterdam, Glens Falls, Albany (New York). I'd race them, and when I'd turn around, they'd be going the other way. It was very satisfying."

But Shirley wanted something more. At eighteen, she entered her first organized drag race at Fonda Speedway in upstate New York. And then, Lebanon Valley Speedway.

"The best thing that ever happened was when Fonda and Lebanon Valley opened their doors," Muldowney said. "We realized then what it was to race under supervision. They provided us with a pot at the end of the rainbow."

But the "pot" was not always filled with riches. As a professional race driver, she sometimes wound up with less money than it cost her to race. That didn't bother her, though. She was doing it for the pure love of the sport. Racing was as much a part of her life as breathing.

Drag racing was still in its infancy in the 1950s. The

Shirley Muldowney

National Hot Rod Association (NHRA) had just held its first championship in 1955.

Muldowney, now a mother, wasn't thinking about winning an NHRA championship at the time—just surviving. She did this by picking up a few dollars here and there at local tracks. She also picked up a nickname. One day she noticed that someone had written "Cha Cha" in shoe polish on her car. The signature nickname stuck with her over the years.

Although Muldowney loved racing, she was always aware of the hazards she faced on the track. "If you don't know what you're doing," she said, "you're in a world of hurt."

She knew the "world of hurt" very well. In the early 1970s she started driving the so-called "Funny Cars." She skillfully handled these tricky vehicles, which often jerked violently on the track. Funny Cars had a shorter wheelbase, full bodies, and—most notably—the engine in front.

In 1973, Muldowney was in a terrible accident. The engine of her Funny Car exploded. The front of the car was suddenly engulfed in flames, spewing fire back at Muldowney in the driver's seat. Fire was all around her. When she emerged, she had suffered severe burns.

"It burned the goggles right off my face."

The accident didn't daunt her spirit. Before long she was back on the track. And heading for the real big time—Top Fuel cars.

Top Fuel cars are the elite of drag racing, the fastest cars in the world. They run on the same explosive nitromethane gas used in rocket engines. From a standing start, these cars are capable of reaching speeds over 300 miles an hour in a matter of seconds. Long and sleek, with the engine behind the driver, Top Fuel dragsters resemble an arrow shot out of a bow once the driver hits the pedal.

But everywhere Muldowney turned, doors slammed in her face. Men refused to race against her. The NHRA refused to give her a Top Fuel license. Even after she finally got her license, race organizers rejected her. Fellow drivers and fans made her life miserable.

"Of course it was because I was a woman," she said. "Toughness got me through it."

She was now a single mom and living in Michigan; she had a new racing partner and crew chief, Conrad "Connie" Kalitta. He had a Top Fuel car built especially for her. Cha Cha took to the tracks in 1974 with her shiny, new pink dragster.

Muldowney wasn't there just to make an appearance. And she wasn't there to be a sideshow as the first woman to race in a professional NHRA event. Not on your life. She was there to burn rubber. She was a *racer*, after all, with a fierce drive to win, and win big.

Her determination paid off. In 1976, she stood in the winner's circle at the NHRA spring nationals. Also during that year, she posted the fastest time and speed of any racer. By 1977, she had won enough such events to gain the

Shirley Muldowney

Muldowney competes in a Top Fuel dragster.

overall NHRA title, known as the Winston World Championship. In three short years, this small 5-foot-4 woman who weighed barely over 100 pounds had out-muscled the other drivers. She had become the top drag racer in the world!

A national car magazine voted Muldowney "person of the year." She was named "Top Fuel driver of the year." The U.S. House of Representatives honored her with an Outstanding Achievement Award. She was on top again in 1980 and 1982. Shirley Muldowney was soon to be a house-hold name, thanks to a movie about her life.

She was riding high. It was June 29, 1984, and Muldowney was ready to start the Grand Nationals in Montreal. She had no idea what an ordeal was ahead of her.

The green light flashed and she gunned the motor. She was off! But something was terribly wrong. The rubber started peeling off the tire and wrapping itself around the spindle of the two front wheels. Usually, the rubber just shreds bit by bit and flies back over the top of the car.

"I had a death grip on that steering wheel because I saw it and I watched it and I did everything I could do," Muldowney said.

She hit the button for the parachute to slow down the car. Too late—by that time the rubber had wound so tightly around the wheels, they exploded. Muldowney's car rocketed off the track, slammed into an embankment, and shattered into little pieces. She had been timed at 247 miles an hour just before the crash.

"It was a very freak accident," Muldowney said. "It only took a half-second to disintegrate."

Muldowney was rushed to a Montreal hospital. She spent two months in the intensive care unit. Five months of operations followed, then a year of therapy. Race again? Out of the question. People wondered if she would be lucky enough to just walk again.

Muldowney was left with a stiff limp and was forced to use a cane. She had trouble climbing stairs.

But at least the horrifying accident had some beneficial

effects. Muldowney's mishap inspired the NHRA to set new safety standards. A charity fund was set up to give financial help to injured racers and their families.

Would Muldowney ever come back to racing? How could she in her condition?

How could she not?

"I love racing so much," she said, "I just had to come back."

And so she did. It was just nineteen months after her terrible accident in Montreal. The year was 1986, and Muldowney was making an appearance in an NHRA event near Phoenix. Her pink dragster was waiting for her, glistening in the sun. She needed help to climb into the cockpit. But she did not need any help after that.

Gunning the accelerator, she roared down the quarter-mile track in 5.58 seconds. It was not good enough to catch the winner, but enough to show she had not slowed down.

It took Muldowney three years to win another NHRA event. When she did, she added another chapter to her comeback story. But that was not the final chapter. Later she starred for the rival International Hot Rod Association (IHRA). She set speed records with the help of a crew that included her son, John, and husband, Rahn Tobler.

Fast forward to 2003. At age sixty-two, Shirley Muldowney, champion drag racer and the First Lady of her sport, had hit the heights and also suffered the lows. The sport she loved had very nearly cost her life. After a legendary career that featured three National Hot Rod Association championships, she made her farewell tour on the drag racing circuit. In her dust she was leaving quite a legacy: Shirley had brought more attention to her sport than anyone in history. She had opened doors for women to compete against men in drag racing, much like Janet Guthrie on the stock car circuit known as NASCAR.

By the time she decided to retire from professional drag racing, Muldowney owned just about every women's record. And some of the men's, too. At one time or another she was the fastest driver on the track. For a long time she was at the top of her sport. She served as an inspiration to other daring young women.

Muldowney understood her place in sports history. One day she was driving to an event when she heard two truckers talking on a CB radio.

"As we're driving along the road I heard one trucker say to another trucker, 'Hey, look up on your left because history is driving by you right there.'

"I thought, 'Wow.' I will never forget that one."

6
BILLIE JEAN KING
Serving One Up For
Women s Rights

The battle was about to begin.

Excitement filled the air as the crowd waited. Slowly the royal procession entered the arena.

The queen appeared first. She sat on a feathered Egyptian throne. She was held high in the air by broad-shouldered men. She smiled and waved to the crowd.

The king followed. Applause and ripples of laughter ran through the crowd. The king was riding in a Chinese rickshaw pulled by beautiful girls.

King wins the women's singles in Wimbledon, 1973.

The king presented the queen with a sweet treat. The queen handed the king a pig. A live pig! He held the squealing animal up high for the crowd to see.

Cheers and laughter rose again throughout the crowd.

And now it was time for the battle.

Roman gladiators in 73 AD? No, just a tennis match in 1973.

Well, not just a tennis match. This was the so-called "Battle of the Sexes"—in many ways a battle for women's equal rights.

Billie Jean King against Bobby Riggs.

Billie Jean King, the queen of tennis, vs. Bobby Riggs, onetime men's tennis champion.

Riggs had another title: king of the "male chauvinist pigs." Like many men at that time, he showed little respect for the female athlete. At least that was his public side. Billie Jean wanted to prove that female athletes deserved respect. She was fighting so that girls would have a chance to realize their dreams.

So it was on September 20, 1973, that Billie Jean King prepared for a tennis match at the Astrodome in Houston, Texas. It was only an exhibition, but it could be the most important match of her life.

Promoters had pulled out all stops. This show of shows had all the makings of a Roman circus with lots of fun and clowning around.

For Billie Jean King, though, the match itself was not funny. It was very serious. Just a year earlier, the U.S. Congress had passed the Education Amendments to the 1964 Civil Rights Act. Under Title IX of those amendments, federal money would equally support female and male school sports programs. Girls now had an open door to their sports dreams. Billie Jean was worried that a loss to Riggs might cause government officials to rethink Title IX.

Even worse, such a loss might deal a crippling blow to the women's movement.

Billie Jean King

A lot was riding on that one event. Millions of people would be watching. Billie Jean hoped she was up to the enormous challenge.

๏๏

Growing up in Long Beach, California, Billie Jean Moffitt was already marching to her own beat. Girls weren't supposed to play football and softball. Billie Jean did—and she was good at both. At the age of eleven, she fell in love with tennis. She worked at odd jobs to save enough money to buy an eight-dollar racket. Dawn to dusk, she was on the court. The slap of the ball against her racket echoed throughout the park.

Every day Billie Jean would walk seven miles each way to school while her classmates took the bus. Why? She wanted to improve her leg strength.

She was excited about her new sport, but there were things about it she didn't like. She hated the bigotry in the tennis clubs. Her black friends were not allowed to play with her on the courts. Billie Jean also hated the sport's old-fashioned attitudes about women. In 1955, she was playing in a tournament at the Los Angeles Tennis Club. Club officials would not allow her to pose for a group photograph with the rest of the girls. The reason? She was wearing tennis shorts instead of a tennis dress. "If I ever got the chance," she later said, "I was going to change tennis and get away from that kind of nonsense."

But first she had to concentrate on her own game. A friend introduced her to tennis star Alice Marble. Billie Jean was delighted when Marble agreed to coach her. "She was so crazy about tennis," Marble said, "I'd have to lock her in her room to study." By the time Billie Jean was fifteen years old, she was ranked nationally and traveling around the country to tennis tournaments.

Win some, lose some. "I was very erratic when I started playing tournaments," she said. The young tennis player was upset and unhappy when she lost. But she decided to learn from her mistakes. She never gave up.

And then, finally her career began to take off. In 1961, Billie Jean and Karen Hantze Susman became the youngest team to win the women's doubles championship at world-famous Wimbledon in London. They repeated that triumph the following year. And to make her star rise higher, Billie Jean pulled off the upset of the 1962 tournament by beating top-seeded Margaret Smith (later to become Margaret Smith Court).

Four years later, Billie Jean won her first Wimbledon singles championship.

Today, winning at Wimbledon brings riches along with fame. The only riches Billie Jean received were a modest gift certificate and some chocolates.

She was now in the big time—without the big money.

"Being a woman athlete didn't mean much in the sixties," she said. "There was no attention, no support, no structure, no money."

Now married to Larry King, a fellow student at Cal State, Billie Jean was headed for the top of her sport. In 1966, it was one success after another: The Wimbledon singles championship. The singles, doubles, and mixed doubles championships at the United States Lawn Tennis indoor tournament at Chestnut Hills, Massachusetts. The South African women's singles championship in Johannesburg. The North of England singles title.

And, she helped lead the United States to a victory over Great Britain for the important Wightman Cup.

In 1968, the United States Tennis Association (USTA) decided to award prize money for its amateur events. Winning Wimbledon now meant a big payoff. For males, that is. Even though the female stars were contributing more and more to the sport, they were still making just a fraction of what the men were making. Billie Jean King refused to accept that kind of inequality.

And what did it take to make her rebel?

The time: September 1970.
The place: The Los Angeles Tennis Club, the organization that had refused to allow a teen tennis player to appear in a photograph in shorts.
The occasion: The Pacific Southwest Open.
The purse for the men's champion: $12,500.
The total *purse for all the women:* $7,500.

Instead of accepting unequal pay, Billie Jean decided to fight the system. She started her own pro circuit—the Virginia Slims tour.

Seven other players joined her. They believed in the tour, if few others did.

"It was a very lonely time," Billie Jean said. "Tough, disappointing, exciting—we had all those emotions."

Billie Jean tirelessly promoted her new venture. She handed out leaflets at street corners. She gave away tickets in front of department stores.

The Virginia Slims tour's success surprised everyone but Billie Jean. In 1971, she made $100,000—the first female athlete to earn that much from her sport in one year. In 1972, *Sports Illustrated* named Billie Jean King its "Sportsman of the Year." Another first for women.

It was a good time for Billie Jean to make her mark. The feminist movement was fighting for equal rights for women in all parts of society.

More and more women were working as doctors, lawyers, and company executives. What a change from previous years, when most people expected a woman to stay home and raise a family.

Billie Jean was making her presence felt in sports. In 1973, a breakthrough! She won her biggest victory off the court: USLTA officials gave in and decided to award equal prize money for women and men in the U.S. Open.

Meanwhile, Bobby Riggs was dreaming up a scheme. Male chauvinists believed women belonged in the kitchen, not on the court. Riggs saw a perfectly good opportunity to make money by promoting a match between himself and a top female player.

Billie Jean King

King prepares to return a serve at a Virginia Slims Tennis Tournament in 1983.

The fifty-five-year-old ex-champion challenged Billie Jean King to a public tennis match. Her answer: no.

So Riggs played Margaret Smith Court, the top-ranked female tennis player in the world.

Riggs easily won the match. It was such a complete rout, it was known as the "Mother's Day Massacre."

Oh, no, King thought, *now I'm going to have to play him.*

It was up to Billie Jean King to defend the women's honor. This was pressure. Some forty million people would watch the event on TV. It was a record for a tennis match.

When she arrived at the Houston Astrodome, Billie Jean was "scared to death."

She knew how important this match was for females throughout the country. She was the underdog. Yet for every girl and woman, she was the symbol of equality. She just *had* to win.

As fate would have it, the match was played in the very same stadium where Billie Jean's brother Randy, a pitcher for the San Francisco Giants, had often played baseball. When she arrived at the Astrodome, Billie Jean went straight to the locker room. She searched for the locker her brother used when the Giants played the Astros in Houston.

Waiting for the match to begin, she sat alone at her brother's locker. She was sick to her stomach. She felt like throwing up.

But in the silence of the locker room, she suddenly felt calm. She felt her brother's presence. She was ready.

When Billie Jean stepped out on the court, she was wearing a blue sequined dress and blue sneakers.

Flashbulbs popped. Music played. Cheers filled the arena as the two tennis players took their places.

"I had a lot of doubts," Billie Jean said. "I didn't have any idea if I could beat him."

But when she stepped on the court, it suddenly became clear. She knew how she was going to play him.

She had to "run him into the ground." Riggs was nearly twice as old as the twenty-nine-year-old Billie Jean. She believed she would have more stamina.

Billie Jean won the coin toss. Her serve.

Billie Jean King

In the first set, Riggs moved ahead, 3–2.

But then the rallies became long. Her plan to run Riggs was starting to work. He was tiring.

First set to King, 6–4.

Riggs told a TV courtside announcer between sets: "She's awful quick and swift. I think I have the balls past her and she gets them."

In the second set, it became obvious her strategy was working. Riggs was having difficulty raising his arm, especially after playing the longest game of the match. He was missing his serves.

After Riggs tied it 3–3, King took over.

Second set to King, 6–3.

Families that had never watched women's tennis before were now watching on TV sets in their living rooms. America couldn't believe what was happening.

King took a 4–2 lead in the third set. But she suddenly felt a cramp in her calf. Nerves? Dehydration? Perhaps both.

Riggs was also having problems. His hands were cramping. Timeout for injury. King and Riggs both received massages.

Back on the court. King went up 5–3. She was one point away from victory. But she was struggling. Same for Riggs. It seemed nobody wanted to win.

Finally, Riggs hit one into the net.

It was over.

Game, set, and match to King, 6–3!

King threw her racquet in the air and extended her arms. A feeling of relief swept through her. It was finally over.

An exhausted Riggs jumped the net and extended a hand.

"You were too good," he said.

The court became a mass of surging people. Suddenly, Billie Jean was being crushed by media and fans rushing to get to Riggs. Boxer George Foreman came to the rescue. He walked down out of the stands and battled his way through the crowd.

"Get away from her!" he shouted as he led King to safety.

Back at her hotel, King celebrated. How? She ordered thirty ice cream sundaes.

How sweet it was! All of a sudden, women's tennis was taking off. The revolution was underway. It wasn't long before women's tennis tournaments were being shown regularly on national TV.

Women would soon receive equal pay at major tennis events. By the nineties, prize money on the women's professional tour had reached a stunning $40 million, with more to come.

Without King, it would be hard to imagine female tennis players among the world's top money earners in sports today.

Many others benefited from King's tireless efforts. She not only helped to start the Women's Tennis Association

(WTA), but also a women's tennis league. And a softball league. She seemed to be everywhere at once. Into a new century she continued to work for women's rights, in and out of sports.

"People still come up to me—men more than women—and say, 'Thank you for what you did for my daughter.'"

7
WILMA RUDOLPH
The Clarksville Comet

ilma Rudolph was waiting.

Waiting to grab the baton...waiting to race into history.

It was the 1960 Olympics in Rome. The American track and field star had already won two gold medals. One more and she would become the first U.S. woman in history to win three golds in the same Olympics.

The AAU awarded Rudolph the James E. Sullivan trophy in 1962.

All she had to do was win the final lap of the 4x100 meter relay race for her team, the Tennessee State Tigerbelles.

Wilma's teammate was running full speed as she completed her part of the race. She reached out to hand off the baton to Wilma.

Trouble.

When Wilma grabbed for the baton, it almost slipped from her fingers. As she desperately struggled to hold on, runners passed her. Finally, she had a firm grip on the stick. By that time, she was in third place behind the German team.

Rudolph took off. Stride by stride, the slender, long-legged runner made up ground. Suddenly, she burst to the front to overtake the other runners. She crossed the finish line by a wide margin over her closest competitor.

The fans were on their feet, roaring. Rudolph had won her third gold medal! She was mobbed by her gleeful teammates. She was overwhelmed with joy and emotion. It was her most satisfying moment on the track.

"Then I could stand on the podium with my teammates, whom I love," Rudolph said, "and we could celebrate together."

൭൫

Coming back to win a race was nothing new for Rudolph. She had overcome numerous hurdles and long odds to become the queen of track. Along the way, she blazed trails for black women in her sport.

At the height of her glory in the '60s, she was known as "the fastest woman in the world." Hard to imagine, considering that as a young girl she was unable to walk.

Wilma grew up in a family of twenty-one brothers and sisters in Clarksville, Tennessee. She was known as the sickly one in the family. Underweight when she was born in

Wilma Rudolph

1940, Rudolph suffered one setback after another. First, double pneumonia, a serious lung disease. Then scarlet fever, which left her housebound. One day five-year-old Wilma woke up and found she had another ailment: her right leg hurt and was twisted inward.

She had been stricken with polio, a crippling virus. It left her limb withered and paralyzed. In the 1940s there was no cure for the disease. Doctors feared Wilma would be severely handicapped for life, or worse, might not survive. They told Wilma she would never walk again. Her mother and siblings thought otherwise.

None of the hospitals near their home admitted blacks. So twice a week, Wilma and her mother boarded a bus for the 60-mile trip to Nashville, the closest city with a hospital that would treat blacks. Well aware that black people were not allowed to ride in the front, they sat in the back of the bus in a crowded section. At the hospital, Wilma took heat treatments and learned how to strengthen her leg with exercises.

At home, Wilma's mother set up a schedule. Each of her brothers and sisters took turns massaging her leg. Three to four times a day, little Wilma, ignoring the pain, would watch her mother and siblings rub her leg. She had to stay at home when her brothers and sisters left for school. School officials would not allow Wilma to attend classes because she could not walk. Someday, she promised herself, she would walk again. Someday, she would be able to join her brothers and sisters in school.

Wilma got around her house by hopping on one foot. She was determined—nothing was going to keep her down. She repeated her exercises again and again each day, no matter how much it hurt. Each day her leg got stronger.

Finally, success! Doctors told Wilma she could walk if she wore a brace. Wilma was overjoyed. She could now join her sisters and brothers in school.

But school was anything but fun. Some of the kids teased her about her heavy steel brace. They made fun of her awkward movements when she walked. Wilma felt miserable. She couldn't even enjoy the sports she loved so much. Wearing the clumsy brace, all she could do was sit on the sidelines and watch everyone else play. Basketball was her favorite. She watched the games hour after hour, longing to step on the court.

Wilma did not give up. At home she continued to strengthen her leg with exercises. She was more determined than ever to walk on her own.

One Sunday she decided to do something daring. Church was already in session when she arrived.

Carefully she took off her brace, steadying herself. Then, with sheer determination, she took her first step forward. She concentrated on one step at a time, placing one foot ahead of the other. Slowly, awkwardly, she walked down the aisle. The church members suddenly became aware of the newcomer. As they stopped to watch, a hush fell over the crowd.

Wilma Rudolph

It was a long walk for Wilma. Step by step, she struggled toward her seat in one of the front pews. Finally, she made it. A wave of relief and exhaustion overwhelmed her as she sat down. The churchgoers were astounded. They believed they had seen a miracle.

Wilma practiced walking without the brace every day. As soon as her leg was strong enough, doctors fitted her with a special high-top support shoe to help her walk without a brace. It was one of the most thrilling moments of her life. At last she was free to play the sports she loved so much. Every chance she got, she was out in the backyard playing basketball with her many brothers and sisters. When the heavy shoe bothered her, Wilma just took it off, tossed it on the sidelines, and played barefooted.

With her long legs, Wilma was able to propel herself through the air. She knew all the moves. She had learned them from watching other kids play on the courts.

Then, soon after Wilma turned thirteen, her doctors pronounced that she was fully recovered. They were amazed. Wilma was not. "'I can't' are two words that have never been in my vocabulary," she said.

Wilma had broken off her physical bonds. Nothing would stop her now. And she had an added motivation.

She hated the way blacks were treated in the South. "I started getting angry about things and fighting back in a new way," she said. "I think I started acquiring a competitive spirit that would make me successful in sports later on."

She turned her anger into an edge. She took to the basketball court with a positive fury, playing harder, jumping higher, and running faster than anyone. She seemed to be trying to make up for lost time.

Wilma went out for basketball at all-black Burt High School in Clarksville. In no time, the little girl who once couldn't even walk without a brace was playing high school basketball. Not only playing, but *starring*. In one season Wilma scored 803 points in twenty-five games. It was a record for girls' basketball in the entire state of Tennessee.

It was not Wilma's ability to put the ball through a hoop that attracted Ed Temple, though. The famous track and field coach at Tennessee State liked the way Wilma ran. He was impressed by the way she sprinted down the track with her long-legged stride. By now Wilma was also a track star winning regularly at the local and state levels.

Temple felt Wilma was special. He was not surprised when she qualified for the 1956 Olympics in Melbourne, Australia. And he wasn't surprised when she brought home a bronze medal for helping her U.S. team to third place in the 400-meter relay.

Wilma was only sixteen, still a high school student. She had grown to nearly six feet. Gangly, with long arms, long legs, and a rail-thin body, she earned the nickname of "Skeeter"—short for mosquito. She was "always buzzing around," said her high school basketball and track coach, Clinton Gray.

Temple wanted Wilma for his team, the famed

Wilma Rudolph

Tigerbelles. Long before she graduated from high school, Wilma's destiny had been set: she was going to Tennessee State on a scholarship. She hoped to add to the legend of the Tigerbelles, one of the great black powerhouses in women's track and field.

Wilma threw herself into track with enthusiasm. Temple loved everything about this devoted runner. He was constantly amazed by her composure. Between races, Wilma took short naps. On the track, she was relaxed and in control. Often she was so far ahead in a race that she slowed down to shout encouragement to her teammates who were further back in the pack.

Not everything went smoothly for Wilma at Tennessee State, though. She missed the entire 1958 season because of illness. In 1959 she was forced to bow out of a meet between the United States and the Soviet Union because of a pulled muscle. In 1960 she became violently sick after having her tonsils removed. But in spite of the setbacks, Wilma qualified for the 1960 Rome Olympics along with other Tigerbelle track and field greats.

Temple was worried that Wilma was pushing herself too hard. When she twisted her ankle in practice the day before her opening race, she didn't let it stop her. She just put ice on the ankle, taped it, and went out to run the very next day.

Wilma survived the three qualifier heats in the 100-meter race. Then she didn't show up for the finals.

"We went crazy," Temple said. "Finally, we found her asleep on the rubdown table in the warm-up tent. Asleep!"

Wilma woke up and won. One gold down.

"After I won the 100…I wondered if my mom and dad were watching because when I left home we didn't have a television. But they were OK. They were able to see me win and see me get on the stand."

Temple worried less about the 200-meter race. It was Wilma's best event.

Rudolph wins gold in the Summer Olympics in Rome, 1960.

Wilma Rudolph

She won. Gold medal number two was hers.

The other Tennessee State runners hadn't had much success individually. They were entered as a unit representing the United States in the 400-meter relay race.

In this race, each member of a team of four runs 100 meters before handing the baton off to the next. Rudolph would run the final lap as the "anchor," usually reserved for the fastest on the team. She was eager for another win, but she wanted the gold medal for her teammates as much as for herself.

"Get me the baton," she told Lucinda Williams, Martha Hudson, and Barbara Jones.

They did. The rest became history.

The first woman to win three track and field golds in one Olympics, she was now a huge international star, adored by millions. Everybody wanted to meet and touch the twenty-year-old woman they called the "Black Gazelle." Some wanted more. A brash fan stole her shoes while she was making her way through a sea of fans in Rome. Wilma stayed in Europe for a while. She gave speeches. She competed. She met the Queen of England.

Back home, Wilma was greeted by cheering crowds. In Louisville, Kentucky, she rode in a pink Cadillac along a parade route. Sitting next to her was her friend Cassius Clay, the Olympic boxing champion who would later be known as Muhammad Ali.

The most important moment of all might have been Wilma's final stop back home in Clarksville.

In her honor, the city had planned a parade and ban-quet—for whites only. Rudolph was angry. She told the planners she would not appear unless blacks were allowed to attend. They bowed to her wishes. Perhaps for the first time in the history of Clarksville, blacks and whites were together at a public event.

Wilma Rudolph had won a victory for equal rights for blacks. She had always hoped to make a difference. This was only the start.

Her widespread exposure as a celebrity brought new prestige to black women in sports. She paved the way for other great ones to follow.

"I don't think people realize how big an influence Wilma Rudolph had on black female athletes," said Bob Kersee, husband of track star Jackie Joyner-Kersee. She called Rudolph her idol.

Rudolph made a difference in other ways.

When she retired from track in 1962, she became the U.S. ambassador of goodwill to French West Africa. She formed a nonprofit organization to help underprivileged children. She remembered when she herself had been an underprivi-leged child.

She also remembered how her family's loving support had helped her fight for a better life. Now as a mother, teacher, and coach, it was only right that she would do the same for others.

8
JOAN BENOIT SAMUELSON
Marathon Woman

O n a warm summer morn-
ing in Los Angeles, Joan
Benoit Samuelson waited to start
the biggest race of her life.

It was a historic moment for
women in the 1984 Olympics. For
the first time, they were running the
marathon in the Games.

"This is the dream," Samuelson
said. "This is the first women's
Olympic marathon."

The gun sounded. The race was
underway...

Benoit poses at her home in Freeport, Maine.

Samuelson got off to a fast start. With short, rapid strides, her
heels kicking high, she widened the gap. By the 3-mile mark she
had surged in front by a large margin.

What was she doing? Marathoners are supposed to pace themselves. They are supposed to save their strength for the long haul.
It seemed she would tire herself out long before the race ended.

LADIES FIRST

She hesitated and thought, "This is the Olympic marathon, and you're going to look like a dodo leading for halfway, and then having everyone pass you."

It seemed like a miracle she was running at all. Three weeks before the Olympic trials, she was forced to have arthroscopic knee surgery. Somehow, she had managed to make it back to run in the Olympics. Not just another race, but a grueling 26-mile marathon.

As it was, Samuelson was running against a far tougher opponent than a field of world-class female runners.

She was battling prejudice.

Most of the people—largely men—who controlled the world of track and field believed that women were not capable of running long-distance races. So-called "experts" thought if a girl ran more than a mile, she would do herself permanent harm. Wrong. And Samuelson was determined to prove it by winning the marathon at the 1984 Olympics in Los Angeles.

Skiing actually came first in Joan's life. It was the natural thing to do during the long, snowy winters of Cape Elizabeth, Maine. Joan was only in third grade when she entered her first race. Skiing halfway down the bunny slope, she was really excited. And she won. "You could see the exhilaration on her face," said her father, Andre Benoit.

In 1974, when Joan was a sophomore in high school, she broke her right leg while slalom racing.

Joan Benoit

The bad news: She had to wear a cast on her leg for ten weeks. When the cast came off, her leg needed exercise. Joan went to the track and started running.

The good news: She found that she loved running as much as skiing.

A year earlier, track and field officials had decided to allow girls to run the mile for the first time. "But if you ran a mile, you couldn't run any other event with the exception of the relay," Joan said. By the time she was a senior, she was running the mile in 5 minutes and 15 seconds! That was only about 45 seconds over the *world* record for women—4 minutes and 29.5 seconds.

But what would people think about a high school girl running long distances? Joan didn't worry about that. "I decided that if I believe in myself, and I'm happy doing what I'm doing, I'm going to go for it."

Long-distance running wasn't Joan's only sport. She also competed in tennis, basketball, and field hockey, a popular women's sport played on grass. But it was as a long-distance runner that she would find her place in sports history.

One day before a field hockey game at Bowdoin College, Joan ran a half marathon. When she showed up to play hockey, she was in bad shape. Joan could barely run above a trot. The coach was not happy. Joan wasn't going to play, not in that condition.

Joan quit field hockey after the season to concentrate on running. She went south and enrolled at North Carolina

State. It had one of the country's top track and field programs. There was one problem.

"I'm a Yankee," she said. "I missed Maine. I missed the ocean."

Back to Bowdoin College. And back to long runs in the pine-filled Maine woods. Joan decided to prepare to run in the famed Boston Marathon. She completed her first marathon in Bermuda in 2 hours, 50 minutes to qualify for the Boston race.

Joan was a senior at Bowdoin, an unknown in the world of marathon running. Her experience was limited. Winning the Boston would mean instant celebrity and worldwide fame.

It was only eight years before in 1971 that women were first officially allowed to run in the Boston Marathon. Before that, there were women who made headlines by running the race on their own, against the wishes of Marathon officials.

Bobbi Gibb unofficially became the first woman to finish the Boston Marathon. Hiding in the bushes in a black bathing suit, Bermuda shorts, and a hooded sweatshirt, Gibb took off after the race started and finished ahead of two-thirds of the male runners. In 1967, Katherine Switzer applied to run in the Boston Marathon under the name of "K. V. Switzer." The Boston Marathon officials gave her a number, unaware that this applicant was a female. About four miles into the race, Switzer was recognized as a female and chased down by an official, who attempted to pull off the number signs pinned to her sweatshirt. Switzer's boyfriend fought back the official, allowing Switzer to finish the race.

Joan Benoit

Now it was the night before the 1979 Boston Marathon. Joan bunked with a friend and ate lots and lots of pasta. "I slept on a mattress on a floor the night before the race," she later said, "and I remember literally rolling into bed feeling stuffed."

While driving to the race, Joan was stopped by a huge traffic jam. So what did she do?

"I just got out of the car and ran through the woods," Joan said. "I must have bushwhacked two miles to the start. I remember thinking, 'I hope I didn't warm up too much.'"

Wearing her college shirt and a Boston Red Sox cap, Joan pulled off the upset of the racing season. She not only won the famed Boston Marathon, she did it in an American record of 2 hours, 35 minutes, and 15 seconds.

It was exciting at first. She made all the headlines. Her phone rang night and day.

"I hated the publicity," she said. "I hated it so much that I seriously considered giving up running so I would be left alone."

Joan considered herself just another resident of Maine. She preferred the quiet life: trapping and cooking lobsters, knitting wool sweaters, and making preserves.

But racing was a hunger that could not be denied. She picked up her pace with a variety of races—two-mile, 800-meter, 10,000-meter, half marathon, and marathon—often setting records.

The demands of marathon running are staggering. Joan had to work through constant pain. Sometimes after a race

Benoit wins the Olympic gold medal for the women's marathon in 1984.

she could not walk for several days. She needed surgery to repair problems with her heels. But she refused to let pain keep her away from the track. No sooner would she peel off the casts than she was back on a bicycle, pedaling with all her might. "Of all the people I have ever coached, she is the most tenacious," said coaching friend Bob Sevene.

In 1983, Joan won the women's division of the Boston Marathon in world-record time—2 hours, 22 minutes, and

Joan Benoit

43 seconds. By the mid-1980s, Joan was regarded as one of the best female marathoners in the world.

After years of doubt that women could run long distances, the Olympic organizers had no choice but to add the marathon for women in the Games.

Now Joan had to make a choice. She had a good idea how much media attention would be focused on the winner. "It was very difficult for me, and I thought, 'I don't know if I can hold up under that again.' Then I decided that I could."

Just a few weeks before the Olympic trials, Joan was forced to stop practice. Waves of pain flooded her right knee. She needed immediate surgery.

No one was sure how long it would take Joan to recover. She put the Olympics on hold. She worked furiously in rehab. A week before the Olympic trials, she still could not walk. Joan kept working. She didn't give up. By the time of the trials, Joan was ready. And she won, gaining a spot on the Olympic team.

She went home to train. She had looked forward to the Olympic marathon for so long, she could hardly believe it was finally a reality. "It took about a month for it to sink in," she said.

Joan was one of the favorites. The field included the eleven fastest women in marathon history. Among them: Norwegian great Grete Waitz, who had won the New York City Marathon five times.

The women were off and running at the 1984 Games in Los Angeles!

∽

The marathon pace had seemed slow to Joan. A lone figure in a white painter's hat turned backwards, she moved ahead of the group. Would she have enough strength to keep up the pace for the full 26 miles?

"I had promised myself I would run my race and nobody else's," she said. No one followed her pace. The other runners thought she was going to burn out before the end of the race, and they would catch her easily. Even the TV commentators were concerned when they saw Joan all by herself so early in the race.

At the 7-mile point, Joan continued her rapid pace. Her lead widened.

By the ninth mile, she was nearly a minute ahead of the field. By the fifteenth, she was almost two minutes ahead.

Waitz made a bid to overtake Joan in the last third of the race. Too late. Joan's big early lead was too much to overcome.

Cruising ahead of the field, Joan saw the huge Los Angeles Coliseum looming ahead. She headed toward the tunnel that would take her into the arena and to a date with immortality.

"Before going into that tunnel," she recalled, "I somehow heard or sensed the crowd inside coming to its feet."

As she entered the tunnel, she was suddenly shrouded in darkness and solitude. Her pounding feet echoed in the eerie silence. She was running toward the light.

Then, a tired thought—the kind that happens when you're so exhausted all you want to do is lie down, curl up, and go to sleep: "I could hide in here and not come out the other side."

Joan Benoit

Of course Joan was not about to hide. Not after long hours of work for the biggest race of her life. Not after her amazing comeback from a knee injury.

She thought: Once you leave this tunnel, your life will be changed forever.

She burst into the arena amidst the roars of 77,000 people. They had been watching her progress on the stadium TV scoreboard and now were cheering wildly as she came into view.

Joan took off her hat. She grabbed an American flag from someone and took her final lap around the track. Only then did she allow herself to smile—a wide, broad smile that said everything.

Her time of 2 hours, 24 minutes, and 52 seconds had wiped out her competition.

Joan was well aware of what she had accomplished.

As the winner of the first Olympic women's marathon, she had achieved the greatest victory of her life—not only for herself, but for women everywhere.

9
SONJA HENIE
The Ice Queen

Henie poses after winning the gold at the Winter Olympic Games in 1932.

She dared not make one mistake.

Sonja Henie, two-time Olympic champion and nine-time world champion, was nervous as she waited to skate onto the ice at the 1936 Games.

She faced the toughest battle of her career. A new challenger was waiting to unseat her as the best figure skater in the world.

In the compulsory figures, Henie had barely managed to win over English skater Cecilia Colledge. It was the closest anyone had come to toppling the Norwegian great.

Henie was entering the free skating competition barely clinging to her lead over Colledge. There were whispers throughout the *crowd: would there be a new champion?*

Dead silence greeted Henie as she skated onto the ice at the Ice Stadium in Garmisch-Partenkirchen, Germany. She was in danger of defeat. How would she respond to the challenge?

☯

It had all started in Norway, the "Land of the Midnight Sun." A little girl named Sonja Henie dreamed of becoming a ballerina. And she did. But she danced on ice, not the stage.

Henie lived in Oslo, the capital of Norway. The country is called the "Land of the Midnight Sun" because it dips into the Arctic Circle, near the top of the world. During the summer, the sun shines all day and most of the night. During the winter, there are only a few hours of daylight, and snow for as far as the eye can see.

The Henie family was rich and owned a lodge outside of Oslo. There, Sonja skied everywhere she could. The charming blue-eyed little girl loved the rhythm of skiing. She loved the feel of the skis, the movement across the packed snow, the wind in her blonde hair. Skiing taught her balance, a skill that would later help her when she became a skater.

Sonja also loved to dance. She studied ballet with Love Krohn, the man who had taught famous ballerina Anna Pavlova.

One Christmas Henie received ice skates. Well, not exactly skates—just a pair of blades she could clamp on her shoes. On her first try, Henie fell on the ice. She fell again. But she would not give up. She found she loved skating more than anything.

After just one year, she won her first figure skating competition. Only seven, she had taken the first steps toward an amazing career: the Pavlova of the ice.

To her skating, she applied the lessons learned from her favorite sports and activities: Balance and rhythm from skiing. Flexibility and graceful moves from ballet.

But Sonja ran into a problem. In those days women skaters wore long skirts to keep them warm in the subzero temperatures of the Norwegian winters. When Sonja went out on the ice wearing the customary long skirt, the wind whipped the skirt between Henie's legs and tossed her in different directions. She couldn't do her fancy new routines.

Her mom came to the rescue. She cut the skating skirt short, above the knees. Then she had another idea. She sewed a border of fur around the bottom of the skirt so it would not blow back or flop around. The problem was solved. Happily, Sonja could now dance on ice.

With her daring new costumes, Henie changed the look of women's figure skating. She was the first to wear silk tights, short white skirts, and white skating boots. They would become her trademark and the talk of the skating world. She was nicknamed "The Girl in White."

But the "Girl in White" could also be the girl in red, or blue, or green.

Not satisfied to stay with the same image, Sonja

constantly tried out new styles. Whenever she took to the ice, she brought the fashion world to skating. She made sure she was dressed for the occasion.

A fellow skater recalled: "The other skaters were in sweaters and skirts. She would show up in a green satin dress with a hat perched on her head at the perfect angle. She never wore the same outfit twice."

The costumes were spectacular, but that wasn't the only thing that made Henie stand out. The main reason she drew so much attention was the way she skated.

At the age of ten, when most kids are enjoying their summer vacations, Henie was hard at work. She went to London to take ballet lessons. With the help of Oscar Holte and other top Norwegian skating instructors, Henie began applying these ballet moves to her skating routines.

Up until then, figure skating hadn't been all that exciting. The women's competition consisted mostly of a boring routine of "figure eights." Skaters were judged on their accuracy as they retraced a path on the ice that resembled the number 8.

The audiences and judges were startled when Henie performed. This skater was different and daring. She jumped higher, spun faster, and lasted longer on her turns than anyone else they had ever seen.

Henie had so many different kinds of spins, it was hard to keep up with them. Would you believe it? Nineteen kinds of spins. Whirling around as many as eighty times. She kept

Sonja Henie

Henie executes a difficult leap in St. Moritz, Switzerland.

viewers on the edge of their seats. She wove a story with her dance movements in her routines. Onlookers were stunned by her agility, energy, and athletic ability.

It had taken a lot of courage for Henie to introduce these colorful dance routines into her ice exhibitions, particularly her jumps. Jumping was generally considered "unfemi-nine" at the time.

Imagine winning the Norwegian ladies skating title at the age of ten. That is just what Henie did. Only a young girl, she was already famous in her own country.

What next? How about the Olympics?

Henie created a lot of excitement when she entered the Olympics in 1924 at the age of eleven. She was much younger than any of the other skaters there. When she stepped on the ice at Chamonix in the French Alps, she introduced her new style of skating. Her routine was so different, no one was ready for it. The jumps, the spins, the creative dance routines—all new.

No, she didn't win. But it made everyone stop and think. A new era had begun in figure skating, and a tiny eleven-year-old girl was leading the way.

She won the world figure-skating championship at the unlikely age of thirteen. It would be the first of ten straight world titles, from 1927 to 1936. She won an Olympic gold medal in 1928, then again in 1932.

Then came the 1936 Olympics and the biggest test of her career.

In the free-skating competition, the outstanding English skater Colledge performed before Henie and had the crowd of 11,000 cheering continuously. Henie knew she would have to give her best to beat her opponent.

Once she was on the ice, her nervousness disappeared.

Dressed in a carefully designed white and violet costume,

Sonja Henie

Henie skated brilliantly. She started with a program of difficult figures and the crowd was with her. Wild cheers followed each routine. She executed a stunning double Axel Paulsen jump, ending in a graceful split. Henie had never skated with more mastery. Her championship was no longer in doubt. She won her third Olympic gold medal.

Olympic triumphs were not enough for Sonja. She had other ambitions. She wanted to be a movie star.

At the time, Fred Astaire was the most famous dancer in Hollywood films. Henie said she "wanted to do with skates what Fred Astaire does with dance."

All of Hollywood had to admire Henie's boldness. Darryl F. Zanuck, head of Twentieth Century Fox, had seen her in an ice show, and he was impressed. Would she like a part in a movie musical? No, she said. She wanted to *star* in her own movie. And she demanded that she be paid like a star. Never mind that it was her first film. Zanuck, one of the most powerful men in Hollywood, bowed to the wishes of this strong-minded 5-foot-2 skater. *One in a Million* and *Thin Ice,* her first two American movies, were box-office hits. Henie was on her way.

During her film career, she shared billing with some of Hollywood's top leading men. Her movies always had a happy ending. And they always featured Henie's dazzling ice-skating routines. She had turned Olympic gold into a sensational career on the silver screen. She became one of the highest-paid movie stars in the world.

There's no telling how many little girls in America fell in

love with ice skating because of Henie. It's possible that young Tenley Albright was one of them. She later became the first American woman to win the world championship and Olympic gold.

When Henie wasn't making movies, she could be seen in her traveling ice show—another first for a figure skater. From 1937 to 1952, Henie toured with her famed "Hollywood Ice Review," playing to sellout crowds. Fans clamored for the Sonja Henie souvenirs sold in the arena lobbies, especially the sparkling costume jewelry pins featuring Henie's image. The audiences usually went home with smiles on their faces.

One time, however, the audience didn't go home happy. Just before the show was about to start, a strange sound came from the stands. Suddenly, the bleachers collapsed, sending hundreds of spectators falling over each other and crashing to the ground.

Everyone rushed to help the victims. A little while later, a stage manager asked Henie, "Shall we start the show now?"

Henie had no intention of going ahead with the show. Instead, she spent the night at the hospital visiting the injured.

With the show, movies, and product endorsements—from fake fur bonnets to face cream—Henie became a money-making machine long before it became the style for athletes. At one point her fortune was estimated at close to $50 million. She was the richest athlete in the world in her time.

Sonja Henie

She was never far from the ice—her first love. When she died in 1969 at the age of fifty-seven, Henie left many fans in mourning. She also left a special legacy.

"She made skating something that every little girl wanted to do," said longtime coach Frank Carroll. "She changed the face of skating. There will never be anyone like her."

Henie's story rivaled fiction. It had everything, including a Hollywood ending.

10
ALTHEA GIBSON
The Jackie Robinson
of Tennis

From the ghetto to greatness.

From the hard concrete pavements of Harlem to the grass courts of Wimbledon, brushing elbows with royalty.

Was Althea Gibson dreaming? Was she really at Wimbledon?

It was the summer of 1957. The place, London, England. The tennis fans at the All England Championships at Wimbledon were excited. There was a buzz in the crowd. The Queen was coming! The Queen was coming! It was a historic first.

Gibson celebrates her victory in the national women's singles championship in 1957.

It was not the only first that day. Gibson was gunning for the singles championship. The historic first? Gibson was black.

The day was steaming hot, over 90 degrees. Gibson walked on to the court wearing an all-white outfit, shorts and a divided skirt.

She was nervous as she faced her opponent, fellow American Darlene Hard.

Gibson had worked long and hard for this moment. She took a deep breath and the match began.

Althea Gibson was born on a farm in South Carolina. The farm failed, and when Althea was three her family moved to West 143rd Street in the mostly black Harlem section of New York City.

Life was not pleasant for Althea. She hated school, but she wasn't happy at home either. Deathly afraid of her father, she often stayed at friends' houses. Sometimes to avoid going home, this little girl rode the city's subways all night long.

When Althea was nine, her life changed. One day barricades went up on her street. No traffic allowed. Her block had been selected by the Police Athletic League as a "play area."

There were games everywhere. Althea played basketball, football, and paddle tennis, as well as the popular New York street game of stickball. And she was good at every sport she tried. For the first time, she was having fun.

When the Athletic League sponsored a competition among all the play streets, Althea won her first medals. She was unbeatable in paddle tennis. One day a supervisor handed Althea a present: a pair of used tennis rackets.

With a tennis racket and her amazing talent, thirteen-year-

Althea Gibson

old Gibson was on her way. Someone mentioned Gibson's name to Fred Johnson, a pro at the New York Cosmopolitan Tennis Club, one of the top all-black tennis clubs in America. "You really have to see this kid. She's amazing!"

Johnson took a look. He liked what he saw. Gibson was a natural. He took her away from the crowded, noisy streets of Harlem, and there in the quiet and private surroundings of the tennis club, he became her teacher. Tall, athletic, and quick on her feet, Althea was a fast learner. Within one year, she was a champion in the American Tennis Association (ATA). It was the beginning of a long string of ATA championships.

A champion, for sure. But still a *black* champion.

The ATA had been formed for African American players because they were not allowed to play in events sponsored by the all-white United States Lawn Tennis Association (USLTA). Tennis had long been the territory of rich white society. What chance would an underprivileged girl have, and an underprivileged *black* girl at that?

Help was on the way. Hubert A. Eaton Jr. and Robert Johnson, two black doctors, felt that Gibson's talent was too great to waste. They had a plan. They were going to make her the Jackie Robinson of tennis.

Robinson had broken the color line in baseball in 1947. The two doctors thought Gibson could do the same in tennis. But there was a catch: Althea would have to leave home. She would have to live in the South, play tennis, and work on her high school diploma.

Althea was frightened to leave the North. Boxing great Sugar Ray Robinson gave her some advice: "No matter what you want to do, you'll be better at it if you get some education." She decided to go.

It was in North Carolina, far from her friendly neighborhood of Harlem, that Gibson discovered racism in its most terrible form.

When she went to a movie theater she was told that she had to sit in the balcony.

When she boarded a bus she was told she had to sit in the crowded back, even though there were empty seats in front.

She couldn't use most public bathrooms or go to restaurants because they were for "whites only."

That was the unfriendly atmosphere that Gibson faced in the South. She was treated like a second-class citizen. She felt sick, as if she had been punched in the stomach.

"You have to be black to understand the nastiness, the stares, the silence," said Eaton.

Gibson refused to give up her dream of becoming a great tennis player. She poured all of her energies into the sport. And she improved her schoolwork. She remembered the advice the great Sugar Ray Robinson had given her about education.

She finished high school and went to Florida A&M University. It took her only three years to earn a degree in health and physical education. She found a job teaching. Amazing—the little girl who had played hooky from school in Harlem was now a college professor!

By this time, she was also the best African American women's tennis player in the country. But even though she was a star in the ATA, the doors of the highly regarded USLTA were still closed to her.

Tennis legend Alice Marble came to the rescue. Marble, who was white, protested Gibson's exclusion from mainstream American tennis. She challenged the tennis association to allow Gibson to face the country's best players. Prodded by the famed and well-respected Marble, the association had no choice but to allow Gibson to play in its events.

In 1950, twenty-three-year-old Althea Gibson became the first black player, man or woman, to compete in the national championships at Forest Hills, New York. Gibson did not win the title, but that competition was the start of many "firsts" for her in tennis:

In 1951, she became the first black, male or female, to play at Wimbledon.

In 1955, she was the first black to be sent on a goodwill tour of Southeast Asia with other top American players.

In 1956, she won the French Open for her first major singles title, another first for a black player.

Winning on the court was one thing. Beating bigotry was quite another. At most matches Gibson sat on the bench next to the tennis court, all alone. No one bothered to talk to her. The white players avoided her.

Gibson makes a return in a 1956 Wimbledon match.

Except at the French Open.

"My coach noticed she didn't have a partner for the doubles, and I didn't have a partner for the doubles," said Englishwoman Angela Buxton. "...I said, 'Why not ask Althea if she'd want to play with me.'"

Buxton teamed up with Gibson to win the French Open doubles title. Then they won the doubles title at Wimbledon.

Althea Gibson

It was a banner year for Gibson in other ways. In 1956, she swept through the tennis world like a tornado: She won the singles championships in the Pacific Southwest tournament. She earned the Pan American, New South Wales, South Australian, Italian, and Asian titles. She was runner-up in the U.S. Nationals.

Gibson's goal now was to be the first black to win at Wimbledon. In 1957 she competed only on grass to get ready for the tournament. She was so focused on Wimbledon that she refused to defend her title in the French Open, which was not played on grass.

At Wimbledon, she was at the top of her game. In the semifinals against British favorite Christine Truman, she crushed her opponent with alarming ease.

Then came the Wimbledon final against Hard, a tough opponent with a strong net game.

@@

Gibson was all over the court. With successful volleys, her nervousness disappeared. She slammed shots to Miss Hard's backhand with such speed that her opponent could only weakly respond. She moved quickly to the net to stop Hard's volleys. Miss Hard shook her head as her errors mounted. First set to Gibson, 6–3.

Gibson was steady and in control. Keep the ball in play and wait for the right shot. In the second set, Gibson's serves jumped quickly off the fast grass court. Hard was having trouble handling the serves. Second set to Gibson, 6–2. The match was over in less than an hour.

"At last! At last!" Gibson said after winning the Wimbledon singles championship.

The Queen came down from the royal box to present the big gold serving dish trophy to the first black tennis player ever to win at Wimbledon.

"My congratulations," the Queen said to Gibson, handing her the trophy for winning the championship at the historic tennis court.

❧❧

Gibson's booming shots, strong play at the net, and brilliant athleticism was the talk of the tennis world. Following another victory in the Wimbledon doubles, she returned to New York for a celebration. She rode in a ticker-tape parade down Broadway. Newspapers and magazines were full of interviews and photos of this new tennis sensation. Everywhere Gibson played, she broke ground as the first black in the tournament. But while the door was opening for Gibson in sports, it was still closed in other parts of American society. In some parts of the country, the welcome sign was not always out for blacks, tennis star or not.

A hotel once refused to make reservations for a group that wanted to honor Gibson at a luncheon. Sorry—no blacks allowed.

When Gibson later broke the color barrier in women's

golf, she faced similar problems trying to integrate that sport. While playing in the Ladies Professional Golf Association (LPGA) tournaments, she was not allowed to use the whites-only clubhouse facilities. Gibson was forced to change her shoes in a parking lot!

Just a couple of months after Gibson's first championship at Wimbledon, a high school in Arkansas became the center of attention in the nation. Little Rock was a big test case in the South for the newly passed integration law. Blacks could now go to the same schools as whites. At least that's what the law said. The governor of Arkansas thought differently. He called up the Arkansas National Guard and sent them to the school. With bayonets drawn, soldiers turned nine black students away from the doors of Central High School. The battle for civil rights was beginning in big cities and small towns across the United States.

At the same time, Gibson continued to rule women's tennis. The U.S. championship followed Wimbledon in 1957. She won both titles again in 1958. She starred for the United States in the famed Wightman Cup series with Great Britain in 1957 and 1958. The Associated Press voted her Female Athlete of the Year for two straight years.

Suddenly, Gibson made a shocking announcement: she was retiring. Despite winning eleven major titles in three years, she could not earn a living from playing tennis. It would be many years before tournaments would begin to award prize money.

She found jobs that paid. She gave tennis exhibitions. She appeared in movies. She sang on TV and made a recording. Gibson played on the women's pro golf tour. And she taught tennis. Still, she had a hard time supporting herself. She eventually dropped out of the public's view.

The next African American woman to win at Wimbledon was Venus Williams in 2000. Venus received $650,000. Match that against the mere trophy that Gibson received for her win in 1958.

It had been a long, hard road, and Gibson's career ended much too soon. She said she was not consciously trying to be a pioneer. She thought of herself as just "a tennis player, not a *Negro* tennis player." But Gibson had opened the door for other black players, both male and female. Among them: Arthur Ashe, Zina Garrison, and Venus and Serena Williams.

In 1988, Althea Gibson presented her Wimbledon trophies to the Smithsonian Institution's National Museum of American History.

"Who could have imagined?" she said at the ceremony. "Who could have thought? Here stands before you a Negro woman, raised in Harlem, who went on to become a tennis player...and finally wind up being a world champion, in fact, the first black woman champion of this world."

This was a dream for Althea Gibson, all right. A dream come true.

11
NADIA COMANECI
The Perfect Gymnast

*I*t was the first night of the
1976 Olympic Games.

*The name repeated by every-
one was Olga, Olga, Olga.*

*Everyone knew about Olga
Korbut. She had dazzled the
crowd and the judges at the 1972
Olympics.*

*Her back-flips had turned her
sport upside down. Suddenly,
gymnastics had become a dynamic
sport requiring speed, power, grace,
and charm.*

*Korbut was the first to bring
worldwide attention to gymnastics.*

*Comaneci stands before her perfect score
in Montreal.*

*Now, four years later, the fans were expecting to be wowed by the
Soviet Union's star once again.*

*Hardly anyone had noticed another name on the program:
Nadia Comaneci.*

Who was Nadia? Just fourteen years old, she was relatively unknown outside of Europe. This gymnast was the mystery element at the 1976 Montreal Olympics.

"I was coming from someplace nobody knew," Nadia Comaneci said.

Nadia was from Romania, a small country in Eastern Europe. She stood just about five feet tall and weighed 86 pounds. The Romanians were the youngest gymnastics team in history to enter the Olympic competition.

Did Nadia and her teammates have a chance against Olga and the powerful Soviet Union team?

⟪⟫

The story had begun years earlier in a kindergarten in Romania.

Two little girls were jumping and doing ballet steps in the playground. They caught the eye of Bela Karolyi, a local gymnastics coach.

Such energy! Karolyi was excited. He contacted Comaneci's mother. The next thing little Nadia knew, she was in gymnastics classes.

The Comaneci household was never the same. Nadia practiced her moves at home, using the couch to cushion her fall. Jump, jump, jump...crack! Another couch on the trash heap. Several couches later, she was still going strong.

"I run, run, run and take off and fly." That was her dream. She discovered she could do this much easier in a gym. She fell in love with gymnastics.

Nadia Comaneci

"I loved being in the air and how it feels, how it feels on your body."

She soon turned into one of Karolyi's hardest working pupils. At the age of seven, she competed in Romania's National Junior Championships and finished thirteenth.

As a present, Karolyi gave her a doll. The doll reminded her not to come in thirteenth again. She didn't.

"She always had a very strong personality, and she always was an achiever," Karolyi said. "She was going to do anything to be the best."

One year later, she won the National Junior Championship.

Nadia had the talent. But talent is never enough. It is the hard work and a willingness to sacrifice that makes a champion.

After school she trained rigorously for three to four hours every day. One day a coach walked into the gym. He watched Nadia complete six 20-second routines in a row. "She wasn't even breathing hard or missing a move on the sixth one," he said.

Nadia's habit was to repeat workouts as many times as possible. That built up her endurance and strength. At the same time, she learned to concentrate on the task at hand.

The years of sacrifice and hard work paid off. The same year Nadia won the National Junior Championship in 1971, she took first place in her first international competition. At age eleven, she became the national champion of Romania.

Then, at age thirteen, Nadia had a surprise for the gymnastics world. At the European Championships, she upset Lyudmila Tourischeva—the outstanding Soviet gymnast who had won the individual championship at the '72 Olympics. Nadia now held the European All-Around Championship title. By 1976, she was ready for her own appearance at the Olympics.

In Montreal, the young Romanian gymnastics team faced fierce competition from the Soviets. Nadia would be competing against champions like Tourischeva and Korbut, but she was well prepared.

In 1972, television had recorded the emotional Korbut's tears and triumphs. In 1976, the media was expecting more great things from Korbut and her impressive Soviet teammates. Olga, with her outgoing personality, was still the crowd favorite as the Olympics began. Nadia was just the opposite. Pale-faced and solemn, she rarely smiled.

Thanks to Korbut, gymnastics had a show-biz quality. Huge crowds attended the gymnastic sessions daily.

The team competition came first. The Romanians were to begin with the balance beam, an event requiring perfect balance and precise movement. This was one of the most difficult ways to start the competition.

It didn't seem to bother Nadia—she scored a 9.9 on a scale of 10.

On to the uneven parallel bars. In this routine, the gymnast leaps from one bar to another—suspended in midair for one thrilling, breathtaking moment.

Nadia Comaneci

The other gymnasts had completed their first-round routines. Nadia was last. Generally in gymnastics, the team superstar performs last. And what a performance it was.

The plan was to psyche the judges with startling new gyrations and an energetic, athletic performance. With her pigtails tied in red and white ribbons, the lithe Nadia attacked the uneven bars. She performed the compulsory pattern with surprising ease. Acrobatically, she swung down from the higher bar and lashed her pelvis to the lower bar. She was in complete control. Once around again, in perfect symmetry. And then, a difficult, twisting dismount from the top of the uneven bars: A high arc, featuring a half twist into a back somersault.

Comaneci performs an excellent balanced jump.

The landing complete, she arched her back like a ballerina's, her arms outstretched to receive the ovation of the crowd.

The routine was so physically taxing that it seemed inconceivable that someone had accomplished it.

Everyone in the arena awaited the judges' score. Nadia and her teammates were stunned.

A perfect 10!

It was a first in Olympic history. It had baffled the computer experts. How would they show a 10 on the scoreboard? The computer wasn't programmed for what was an "impossible" score. "Because of the gasps around the arena, I looked around and saw the 1.00 on the scoreboard and didn't understand what was happening," Comaneci said. But when the crowd saw the 1.00 flashing on the scoreboard, they knew. Suddenly the fans were on their feet, cheering. This time, Comaneci—the girl who never smiled—extended her hand, waved and smiled. Millions of television viewers around the world tuned in for the second night of the team competition. It was billed as the battle between Nadia and Olga.

Could Nadia make history again?

Korbut opened with a strong performance on the uneven bars, her favorite. She repeated her now-famous risky back flip off the high bar to squeals of delight from the audience.

Her score: 9.90.

Comaneci didn't seem flustered. She calmly mounted the dangerous balance beam. She flipped and twisted, drawing oohs and aahs from the crowd.

Another perfect 10 from the judges.

Unbelievable. Nadia had done it again. A perfect 10!

Korbut was struggling. Comaneci was surging. She received a 9.85 in the floor exercise, another 9.85 in the vault.

Back to the uneven bars. The capacity crowd of 16,000 at the Montreal Forum waited to see Nadia's performance. The only sounds heard were hundreds of cameras clicking as she made her incredible moves.

Would the tough international judges who had never given a 10 before in any previous Olympics give two perfect scores on the same night? And to the same gymnast?

Utterly impossible, everyone thought.

Front flips...twists...a dramatic dismount.

Her performance was flawless. The score flashed on the board: 1.0.

Nadia had done it again! Her third perfect 10.

The upstart new kid on the block from Romania was stealing the spotlight from Korbut. Nadia came close to stealing the team gold medal from the Soviets. Because the score is based on overall team performance, the Soviets won the gold. Nadia and her teammates won the silver.

But Nadia remained the center of attention that night. The crowds applauded and cheered, forcing Nadia to come back twice on the floor. She smiled and waved at the adoring fans.

The fourteen-year-old was taking everything in stride. Everyone seemed more excited over her history-making achievement than Nadia. Her reaction was typically calm: "I was really glad and I felt really good. I think I've done well."

Next challenge for Nadia: the individual competition. Despite her three perfect scores, she was still looking for the gold. The winner of the individual events would not only take home a gold medal but would also be recognized as the best all-around female gymnast in the world.

Comaneci was young, so young. This was her very first Olympics. She was going to perform on the biggest athletic stage in the world. And she was facing incredible competition from Olympic veterans who were several years older.

Comaneci was an athlete unafraid of dangerous moves. But could she beat the world's best for her first Olympic gold medal?

"She has no fear," said Bela Karolyi, her coach.

"She can block out the whole world," another coach said. "It's just her and the apparatus." Her power of concentration was never more apparent than that night at the 1976 Olympics.

She rarely watched other performances. She kept herself busy with warm-up exercises. She chalked the bar for her own routines.

Before going through her exercise she stood in front of the apparatus for what seemed like an eternity. Everything had to be perfect. Was the crowd quiet enough? Was the bar chalked up enough? Were her feet and hands in the right position?

A standing-room-only crowd of 18,000 filled the Montreal Forum. Anticipation was high as the thirty-six all-around finalists walked into the arena. Everyone was waiting. Would Comaneci be able to handle the pressure? Would one of her daring somersaults or double twists produce a fall? Would she be able to score another history-making 10?

She was registered in four events in the individual competition—uneven parallel bars, balance beam, vault, and floor exercises.

In 1976, the winner of the all-around individual title was determined by average scores from both the team and individual competitions.

Comaneci was eligible for a medal in all four events in the individuals.

On the uneven bars, she charged into new territory with front flips and twists and a spectacular dismount. It took imagination and nerve. The dismount was eventually named after her. It's known as the Salto Comaneci dismount. Her routine on the bars was seemingly so reckless that one Olympic official said it should be banned.

The tough international judges had little choice.

The judges' decision: a perfect score.

The balance beam?

Another 10.

Also, Nadia scored a 9.85 in the horse vault and a 9.9 in the floor exercise.

Comaneci won the Olympic gold medal as the top all-around gymnast in the world! Korbut finished a disappointing fifth.

Before the Olympics were finished, Comaneci was awarded two more perfect scores. Her grand total: seven.

Comaneci won three gold medals in Montreal. She added two more at the Moscow Games in 1980. From 1976 to 1984 she won an astounding twenty-one gold medals in Olympic and world championship competition.

Now she seemed to have it all—fame and admiration. But she was not happy. Her country was under oppressive Communist rule. The people were not free like they are in the United States or other democratic countries.

So Comaneci made the biggest leap of her life. She escaped from Romania in 1989. Her destination: America, land of the free. Bela Karolyi, her old coach, had defected earlier.

Time has not dulled her fame. In a 1999 poll of international journalists, Comaneci was voted the Top Female Athlete of the Twentieth Century.

What's more, her historic feat in Montreal may never be topped.

"I think she's the best gymnast the world has ever known," said Frank Bare, executive director of the United States Gymnastics Federation.

Nadia would never again be an unknown.

12
MANON RHEAUME
Manon the Warrior

All alone.

A female warrior waits to meet the enemy.

Her name is Manon Rheaume.

Dressed in armor, an iron mask shielding her face, she glances at the weapon by her side.

She is preparing herself mentally for the challenge ahead of her. She is on a quest to do what has never been done.

Manon Rheaume at a 1992 news conference.

Feelings of excitement rise from the pit of her stomach as she visualizes the battle. Alone, surrounded by ice, she must use her weapon, her skill, her arms, her legs to defend her fortress.

The enemy will try to invade using a missile flying at great speeds. She must stop the missile at all costs, or lose the battle.

LADIES FIRST

The battleground is a hockey arena. Rheaume is a goaltender. She is about to make history as the first female to play in a men's professional hockey game. It is the highest level of hockey—the National Hockey League.

September 23, 1992. Rheaume stands waiting with her Tampa Bay Lightning teammates behind her to take the ice. A near-sellout crowd of 8,223 fills the Florida State Fairgrounds Expo Hall for the exhibition game against the St. Louis Blues.

Will she embarrass herself? Will she let her team down? She's feeling the pressure and her nerves are starting to jangle. Is she just there as a publicity stunt? Are they right? Is she too small, too fragile to play at the top level? Rheaume has been in many high-pressure hockey games before, but never against this kind of competition. She will face blazing shots at 100 miles an hour. And the game will be quicker—much quicker than anything she has been used to.

This game would be faster, rougher, and more violent. Her calm exterior doesn't show the nervousness that is slowly enveloping her.

The organ music breaks into her thoughts. Then, the announcement:

"Ladies and gentlemen, YOUR Tampa Bay Lightning!"

And there she is, leading her team out on the ice to the thunderous cheers of thousands.

As starting goaltender, the warrior takes her place in the net and awaits her first shot...

Manon Rheaume

Breaking barriers was nothing new for Rheaume.

She had been playing goalie since she was five years old. She lived in a small Canadian town outside of Quebec City. At first she played against her older brothers.

"When I was young, in our house downstairs, we put up a goal and a net," Rheaume said. "I would dress up in all the equipment and they would shoot on me."

Rheaume learned all about hockey. The game is played on the ice. The players can skate backward or forward at incredible speeds with equal skill. They use long sticks with broad blades to move an object called the puck up and down the ice. The three-inch puck is round and made of hard, black rubber. It resembles a big frozen Oreo cookie without the cream in the middle. In the National Hockey League, it can travel at speeds up to 100 miles an hour.

As the last line of defense, the goaltender is the most important player on the ice. With a blocker and a big-bladed stick, it is the goaltender's job to stop the opposing team from shooting the puck into the net. Sometimes the goalie uses parts of his body to block the puck.

The goalie is well padded from top to bottom, wears leg shields and a metal helmet with a mask to protect against serious injury. This doesn't mean the goaltender will be safe.

Goalies are bumped. Run into. Run over. And that is only the beginning. They face grave dangers from speeding skaters—and speeding pucks. Goaltending is the most dangerous position in hockey.

Manon Rheaume waits her turn to take the ice as goaltender.

Rheaume's father was a tough hockey coach. He never spared her feelings. She learned to be strong and resourceful. She would never be a crybaby. She would never be a quitter.

Manon played many sports, but hockey was her passion. She grew older. There weren't many opportunities for girls to play hockey. She played against the boys.

Rheaume was a really good player. Sometimes better than the boys. That posed some difficulties when she played on boys' teams.

"Parents were jealous and thought their little boys would make it to the NHL," Rheaume said, "so they thought I didn't deserve the chance to play."

Rheaume thought differently. She continued to practice

and play like her hero, all-star goaltender Patrick Roy, a Montreal native. She copied Roy's "butterfly" goalie style: dropping to his knees and spreading his feet sideways to cover more area of the net.

She took her game to the Canadian Major Junior Hockey League. This league is a steppingstone to the NHL for teenagers—teenage boys. The competition was considered too tough for a girl.

Too tough for most girls. Not for Rheaume.

She was the first female to play in Canada's top amateur league. Her team: the Trois-Rivieres Draveurs.

Game time. Manon the Warrior strapped on her battle gear. She took her place in the net for the Draveurs.

She tensed for a shot. The speeding puck came at Rheaume at eye level. Before she had a chance to react, it slammed into her mask. She reeled backwards from the impact.

Suddenly, she saw blood. A cut had opened near her right eye. Somewhat dazed, she steeled herself, ready to play. She refused to leave the game.

Finally, the blood took its toll. Her vision blurred. She couldn't see. She was forced out of the game.

"My mask looked like it had been in a car accident," said Rheaume, who received three stitches.

The team doctor said that most other goaltenders would have dropped to the ice after receiving such a blast. Yet Rheaume continued to play.

At the time she was on the Draveurs, Rheaume was also playing for Canada's national women's team. In 1992 she led the Canadians to the gold medal at the world championships in Finland. The gold medal attracted attention.

Phil Esposito, general manager of the Tampa Bay Lightning, sent Rheaume an invitation. "Try out for the Lightning," he challenged.

Unbelievable. An impossible dream.

The 5-foot-6, 135-pound Rheaume would be the first female to compete in one of the four major professional sports: major-league baseball, football, basketball, and hockey.

The challenge was out there. The question was, should she accept?

Did she really have a shot at making an NHL team? Or would she be just a publicity stunt, a circus sideshow?

Should she accept the challenge? The pressure would be enormous.

Finally, she said yes.

"I decided I didn't want to look back in ten years and be sad that I didn't go to Tampa Bay," Rheaume said.

The twenty-year-old Rheaume showed up at the Lightning training camp. So did the media. She was like a rock star in skates. In one eleven-day period, she did a hundred interviews!

"I'm having a hard time relaxing and getting good sleep," she said.

Manon Rheaume

She didn't receive, nor expect, any favoritism just because she was a female. Lightning coach Terry Crisp told it as it was:

"The guys out there are all trying to make a living. They can't afford to pull up on their shots. And in the heat of the battle, nobody is going to take time to decide if it's a guy or a girl in the net. She's just a goaltender."

That was fine with Rheaume. She felt she was there for more than just the publicity.

"I don't face 100-mile-an-hour shots everyday and I don't have bruises everywhere on my body to have publicity," she said.

A hamstring and groin injury couldn't stop her. She played through agonizing pain as she blocked blazing shots.

Training camp was tough. Players were cut. But after the first few weeks she was still there.

"I haven't been an embarrassment," she told reporters.

The impossible dream came true. Rheaume would start in the exhibition game against the Blues.

Now the historic moment had come. Rheaume didn't have long to wait for her first shot. Just 40 seconds into the game at the Florida State Fairgrounds Expo Hall, Rheaume stopped a slap shot for her first save.

"It was important to stop it," she said. "After that, I relaxed. I wasn't so nervous."

Then she stopped another shot, kicking the puck away with her right leg pad.

But another shot got by her.

"It was a bad goal," she said. "But even good NHL goalies give up bad goals."

Rheaume soon had a chance to redeem herself. One of the Lightning players broke a rule and was sent to the "penalty box." This gave the Blues a "power play," meaning they had one more skater on the ice than the Lightning. Tampa Bay was playing "shorthanded," a scary situation for a goalie.

The Blues have the puck. Here they come, steaming down the ice, steaming toward the goal that Manon is guarding. Manon tenses. Suddenly a player breaks free right in front of her. He has Manon at his mercy.

He pulls his stick back for a hard shot. He fires toward the upper right side of the net.

GOAL!

But just when it seems certain the puck is going to fly into the net, Rheaume slides across the goalmouth to snare the shot with her glove.

NO GOAL!

The crowd goes wild. The scoreboard flashes the words in capital letters: AWESOME, AWESOME!

With Manon's help, the Lightning had killed the Blues' power play.

Manon Rheaume

Manon gave up a goal before leaving at the end of one period. The game was tied at 2. She had faced nine shots, made seven saves.

"She surprised me like she surprised everyone," said Tony Esposito, the Lightning's director of operations and a Hall of Fame goaltender.

The performance convinced the Lightning to offer Manon a contract with its top minor league team in Atlanta. Over the years she had moderate success while playing on different levels of professional hockey.

Then it was back to the Canadian women's national team and an appearance in the 1998 Olympics. Another goal realized. The Canadians went on to win the silver medal.

By then Rheaume was the most famous female hockey player in the world. She had shown the way for other women like Hayley Wickenheiser, the first female to score a point in a men's professional hockey game.

"When you have a dream," Rheaume said, "you want to go after that dream."

Manon Rheaume had become a legendary warrior.

13
THE ALL-AMERICAN RED HEADS
A Team of Their Own

HE PINCHED ME! HE PINCHED ME!" *the redhead screamed, pointing at the opposition basketball player.*

The referee's shrill whistle split the air. Five redheads suppressed giggles as an amused audience witnessed the drama on the basketball court.

The All-American Red Heads in the 1950s

LADIES FIRST

"Foul, most foul," the referee declared.

An embarrassed male player stood there, protesting.

"She pinched ME!" the player insisted. No one was listening.

The redheaded basketball player stepped to the line to shoot her foul shots—on her knees! The spectators chuckled.

Down went the player. Up went the basketball.

Score!

One more time.

Score again!

Everyone laughed and cheered.

The All-American Red Heads had come to town.

In red, white, and blue uniforms, this remarkable women's basketball team packed gymnasiums in small towns and drew crowds to big city arenas.

Red, white, and blue—and razzle-dazzle.

They were many years ahead of their time. They blazed a trail for women's basketball long before it became nationally popular in the eighties and nineties.

Before colleges started seriously supporting women's sports, thanks to the Title IX legislation in 1972, there were the Red Heads.

Before the U. S. women's team won a gold medal in the Olympics of 1996, there were the Red Heads.

Before Sheryl Swoopes, Rebecca Lobo, and Lisa Leslie made headlines playing in the Women's National Basketball Association, there were the Red Heads.

The All-American Red Heads

The All-American Red Heads paved the way.

And what a show they put on!

The crowds had never seen two girls dribble four basketballs at one time. They were amazed when a Red Head bumped the basketball into the hoop with her head.

And just as amazed when a Red Head stood on her head and shot the basketball into the hoop with her feet. Or balanced two basketballs on her knees.

It was fun, fun, fun.

Sure, they could do tricks, but they could also play some serious basketball. Make no mistake, they had "game." They were skilled professional basketball players as well as entertainers.

They played mostly men's teams under men's rules. And they usually won. What a blow for the male ego!

"A lot of times, the men came in expecting a bunch of girls they could push around," Mickey Childress said. "But we were in good condition."

Childress played for the Red Heads in the 1960s. "Our first quarter was pure basketball," she said. "We wanted to show the public that we knew how to first of all play basketball."

The rest was pure entertainment.

The Red Heads were a long-running hit, too—lasting for a full fifty years, from 1936 to 1986.

"We like to think we helped women's basketball stay alive when the colleges weren't playing our game," Childress said.

❀

It had all started in Missouri in the 1930s. The setting: a beauty parlor. The main characters: two beauticians.

They happened to be on a basketball team sponsored by the beauty parlor. They also happened to be redheads. And so, the idea for a prank.

They convinced their teammates to join in. What did they do? They shocked the fans.

When they walked out on the basketball court for the game, the crowd saw red. Redheaded guards. Redheaded forwards. A redheaded center. Every single player on the team had dyed her hair red.

They were walking advertisements for the beauty parlor they worked for, and a big hit with the fans.

Come out and see the Red Heads play!

The prank was so successful, the following year the "Missouri Red Heads" were touring and attracting big crowds. C. M. Olson and his wife, Doyle, the beauty parlor owners, had founded an American original.

Every season was an adventure for the Red Heads. It was the 1940s, just before World War II. The Red Heads were visiting the Philippines. Suddenly, the State Department issued a warning to leave as quickly as possible. For a while, the girls seemed to be stranded. A cattle boat came to their rescue, and they were escorted out of the area by a Navy minesweeper. In the 1940s, many of the team members left

The All-American Red Heads

the road to work in airplane factories and support the war effort.

AAU All-Americans began joining the team. The team was renamed. The *All-American* Red Heads were born.

In 1955, coach Orwell Moore bought the team and moved the Red Heads to Caraway, Arkansas. He operated the franchise with his wife Lorene, a former player, until the team's last year in 1986.

Childress was a freshman in high school in Gate City, Virginia, when the Red Heads came to town. Basketball was her first love. When she saw the fun and the skill on the court, she knew right then that's what she wanted to do.

So she approached the coach after the game. "I want to play for the Red Heads," the bold teenager said.

The Red Heads' coach condescendingly patted her on the head. "If you keep practicing, maybe you will someday."

Childress now had a dream to follow. She starred in high school, where she broke a Virginia school record for points in a game. She later played for the University of Tennessee.

Childress's heroics attracted attention. An offer came from the Red Heads: two hundred dollars a month plus expenses.

"It wasn't a great deal of money," Childress said, "but to play basketball and get paid for it was the greatest thing to come down the pike."

A hard worker, Childress was not going to go unprepared. She trained all summer with an NBA player.

"I thought I was in great shape," she said.

She had second thoughts when she started training with the Red Heads.

The workouts were strenuous and intense.

"About the third morning after I got there, I had no idea that everything you owned could be sore at one time—including my eyelids.

"When we got up and finally got dressed and got to the door, the station wagon had already left for breakfast. It was a long time to lunch and a lot of activity left. As we stepped outside our motel rooms, there lay a jump rope for everyone."

It made Marine boot camp seem like a walk in the park.

Things didn't change during an exhausting barnstorming season, which started in the fall and ended in the spring.

Traveling in a station wagon on a trip covering thousands of miles, they would play some 200 games. They played in a variety of cities, on college campuses, Indian reservations, and military bases. They took on American Legion teams, Lions Club teams, high school graduates.

For a full half century, a variety of Red Head teams—sometimes as many as three at a time—barnstormed around North America.

What a whirlwind! Childress's days were spent on the road in the team's old green station wagon—three in the front, two in the middle, three in the jump seat.

Every once in a while, the station wagon would make an "R and R" stop. Rest and recreation? No, roadwork and more roadwork. The players would race each other—wind sprints between telephone poles with cries of "Go, girl, go!" ringing into the air.

There were snowy, freezing days. When the station wagon got stuck, the Red Heads piled out and pushed. One time after a game in Vermont, a car window had frozen in the down position. As the Red Heads pulled away from the arena, some pranksters fired snowballs through the window. Laughing and covered with snow, the Red Heads finally made their getaway.

The trusty old station wagon was a key player in the Red Heads' travels.

"We put our luggage on top. In the wintertime a tarp went over the top. No one wanted to be the last one to put her suitcase on top. That meant you had to put the tarp up."

The Red Heads had to wash their own uniforms.

"They were heavy," Childress said. "And I played many times in a cold, wet uniform that just didn't get dry between games."

But the overall experience was wonderful for Childress, as it was for hundreds of other Red Heads.

In 1959, Ella Cross was a Tennessee teenager who had only played half-court in high school. That year the Red Heads recruited her, and she was called to join the team on the road.

The basketball game was already underway when Cross finally arrived in Poplar Bluff, Missouri. She was

The All-American Red Heads with coach Orwell Moore in 1955

exhausted following her 560-mile journey. Exhausted, yes, but not too tired to play.

Ella soon had her first taste of professional basketball action. It was midway through the first quarter when the coach sent her into the game.

The teenager felt lost, and it wasn't only because she was so far from home.

"Can you imagine being introduced to five redheaded girls and trying to remember their names?" Cross recalled of that night. "I didn't know who could shoot. I didn't know who to throw it to. So I just shot it."

The nineteen-year-old from Oneida, Tennessee, made quite a debut. She scored 27 points for the All-American Red Heads.

The All-American Red Heads

Cross had never done any fancy ball handling. She quickly learned to juggle three balls, shoot free throws with her back to the basket, and spin the ball on her fingertips.

Shooting from unusual positions was normal for the Red Heads. A favorite was the "Old Piggy Back Play," where one player climbs onto the shoulders of another and drops the ball in the basket.

The play had been dreamed up by a pair of early Red Head stars—Gene Love and "Stubby" Winters. Love, 6-foot-4, was nicknamed "Careless Love," after a popular song. Winters was only 5-foot-4, but she didn't let her short stature hamper her performance.

As a matter of fact, it worked to her advantage when the Red Heads put on their famous "Dribbler Through Act."

Love, a center, sets up with her back to the basket, legs planted wide apart. Winters grabs a pass from a teammate.

Dribbling the ball with an opponent in pursuit, she ducks through Love's legs and goes for the basket. Her opponent tries to follow. Big mistake. He is trapped by Love's long legs.

Winters has an easy basket.

And the bounce goes on…

Fast forward to 1999. The Women's Basketball Hall of Fame opened in Knoxville, Tennessee, and some seventy-five Red Heads walked through the door. They were there to be honored as a team with other women's basketball greats. Among them: Senda Berenson, "The Mother of Women's Basketball," who first established the game at Smith College in the 1890s; Nancy Lieberman, first woman to play in a men's professional league in the 1980s; and Ann Meyers, who was invited to training camp with the Indiana Pacers of the NBA, although she never played a game.

"We had a reunion at the Hall of Fame," Mickey Childress said. "We had members of the first team and members of the last team. You cannot imagine the family we were."

Among the early Red Head greats attending the Hall of Fame opening were Charlotte Adams and Red Mason.

So what did they do? They entertained. The Red Heads started doing their old tricks with a basketball.

"The Red Heads had everybody, including the vendors, out dancing," Childress said.

Walking through the Hall, the Red Heads spotted a familiar friend: an old, green station wagon with "Moore's All-American Red Heads" imprinted on the door. Once discarded in an Arkansas field, it had been brought back to life, a reminder of days gone by for a group of female pioneers.

They may have been born with blonde, brunette, or black hair, but in their hearts they would always be Red Heads.

CONCLUSION

By the early 1900s women were pushing harder and harder against the boundaries society had set for them, and in 1920, they finally won the right to vote. Female athletes continued to push, too, breaking down people's stereotypes about women in sports.

During World War II, women pitched in. They came out of the kitchen and into a man's world. They managed businesses; they drove trucks. They worked in factories, building airplanes. Then they flew them, transporting supplies all over the globe. They did everything but fight.

At home they helped to keep up morale by filling in for the male athletes who had been called to the battlefield. While the All-American Red Heads were drawing crowds to basketball arenas all over the country, women were pitching, catching, and hitting on the baseball diamond as part of the All-American Girls Professional Baseball League.

During the fifties and sixties, women athletes like Althea Gibson and Wilma Rudolph not only opened the door for other young black women in sports but also used their celebrity to bring public attention to the struggle for civil rights.

In 1972, Title IX of the Education Amendments Acts was passed, prohibiting all schools and universities that received federal funds from discriminating on the basis of sex. Women's college sports expanded during the next few years, and girls gained more and more opportunities to play sports at a much higher level. Women, once excluded from the Olympics, were making their presence felt at the Games, showcasing their amazing physical skills and attracting worldwide attention. Female superstars in sports such as tennis and gymnastics were idolized by both men and women across the country.

Through the last decades of the twentieth century, female athletes continued to break new ground by competing at high levels in many sports that had been dominated by men. Women ran the marathon. Women jockeys took honors in the most prestigious races. Committed and hard-working females kept breaking gender barriers in sports. Some of these remarkable women are listed below:

∞ 1953: Toni Stone, first woman to play baseball in the Negro League

∞ 1978: Janet Guthrie, first woman to complete the Indianapolis 500

∞ 1985: Libby Riddles, first woman to win the Iditarod dog sled race in Alaska

Conclusion

👁👁 1985: Lynette Woodard, first woman to play for the Harlem Globetrotters

👁👁 1986: Nancy Lieberman, first woman to play in men's professional basketball

👁👁 1989: Julie Croteau, first woman to play NCAA baseball

👁👁 1992: Lyn St. James, first woman to compete in a men's professional racing league

👁👁 1997: Ila Borders, first woman to play in a men's professional baseball game

👁👁 2002: Katie Hnida, first woman to play in a Division I college football game

The women in this book weren't necessarily trying to be trailblazers.

All they wanted to do was participate in a sport, and play it as well as they possibly could. But these First Ladies of Sports, with their courage, perseverance, and dedication, have not just become a part of sports history, they have made a lasting contribution to society.

These women are all winners who made a difference.

Bibliographical Note

Along with personal interviews, I used a number of newspaper and magazine sources to research this book. I relied most heavily on the Associated Press, *Chicago Tribune, Los Angeles Times, New York Times, Washington Post, Sports Illustrated,* and *Sports Illustrated for Kids.* I also found helpful the Current Biography Yearbook series available in most libraries, as well as some of the leading internet sites.

If you want to learn more about these athletes and other women in sports, you may find the following books of interest.

Althea Gibson, by Tom Biracree

America's Champion Swimmer: Gertrude Ederle, by David A. Adler

Babe: The Life and Legend of Babe Didrikson Zaharias, by Susan E. Cayleff

LADIES FIRST

Female Firsts in their Fields: Sports and Athletics, by Ann Graham Gaines

Figure Skating to Fancy Skating, Memoirs of the Life of Sonja Henie, by Michael Kirby and Scott Hamilton

Joan Samuelson's Running for Women, by Joan Benoit Samuelson and Gloria Averbuch

Letters to a Young Gymnast, by Nadia Comaneci

Manon: Alone in Front of the Net, by Manon Rheaume and Chantal Gilbert

Outstanding Women's Athletes: Who They Are and How They Influenced Sports in America, by Janet Woolum

Riding for my Life, by Julie Krone and Nancy Richardson

Shirley Muldowney's Tales From the Track, by Shirley Muldowney and Bill Stephens

Sports Hero, Billie Jean King (Sports Hero Biographies), by Marshall Burchard and S. H. Burchard

Susan Butcher and the Iditarod Trail, by Ellen M. Dolan

Wilma Rudolph (Black American Series), by Tom Biracree

Winning Ways: A Photohistory of American Women in Sports, by Sue Macy

Women's Sports: A History, by Allen Guttman

About the Author

ongtime sports writer Ken Rappoport is the author and coauthor of dozens of books for young readers and adults, including PROFILES IN SPORTS COURAGE; MIRACLES, SHOCKERS, AND LONG SHOTS; HARVARD BEATS YALE 29-29 AND OTHER GREAT COMEBACKS FROM THE ANNALS OF SPORTS; GRIDIRON GLORY; and biographies of Wayne Gretzky and Shaquille O'Neal. Ken has written about the NCAA basketball championship, minor league baseball, college football rivalries, and numerous teams and their players. He received a national award from *Writer's Digest* for a profile on St. John's basketball coach Lou Carnesecca.

At the Associated Press, Rappoport covered every major sport out of New York for thirty years and was the AP's national hockey writer for fourteen years. He covered the World Series, NCAA Finals, Olympics, NBA Finals and Stanley Cup playoffs, among other events.

Ken lives in New Jersey.

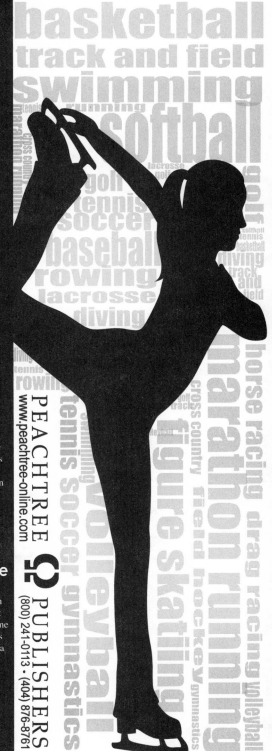